SAYING YES

An International Love Story

PATRICE LEFEBVRE

Dedication

To my husband, best friend, and love of my life.

Thank you for asking me to dance, for all of your incredible support, and for 'being not afraid' to love full out.

Contents

Acknowledgements

I would like to thank my writing teachers in the U.S., Canada, and on the magical Internet.

Many thanks to my parents for so many things, but especially for introducing me to the wonders that live between book covers and the value of saying *YES!* to life.

Special thanks to my extraordinary writing group partners, Bernice, Bronwen, and Leanna, for your patience and guidance, your willingness to read multiple drafts of these chapters, and for generously giving insightful and gentle feedback.

In addition, my gratitude goes out to the following wonderful women who offered to read and provide valuable ideas and encouragement: Barbara Felong, Geri Dent, Lauren L'Amour, Moira Farr, Nicole Mignone, Shelley Arenas, and Vickie Laurie.

Without your caring support, this book would never have been completed.

Chapter 1

November 2008

It wasn't my alarm clock, but a mechanical *pwew-pu* from the computer speakers that woke me. The sound announced one of two things, either Pierre had readied himself for work without waking me and then disconnected, or – as too often happened – Skype had dropped the call. In the dim light of the screen, the clock read 1:15 AM, 4:15 in Ottawa, far too early for him to head to work. A familiar weight settled as I realized I was alone again. His soft, rhythmic snores through the computer on the bedside table didn't fool me into believing he was there, but, like a lullaby, his night sounds soothed me to sleep and diminished the missing-him blues. Now again, the speakers were silent.

Sighing, I pulled up the covers and let my mind drift, hoping to slide back to sleep. I tried to focus on the white-noise patter of perpetual rain against the window, but my incessant monkey-mind thoughts interrupted. We wouldn't talk again until the following evening, mine early, his late. The coast-to-coast time difference was a pain but faded to near insignificance when compared to the distance itself.

You would think I'd know better. Carrying on a long-distance relationship at my age was so impractical. My days were jammed with running to and from the real estate office, making requisite phone calls, attending classes, driving to showings, and meeting with hopeful potential home buyers, sellers, or competing agents. The slowdown in U.S. home sales months earlier had coincided with my divorce's final signing and didn't equate to fewer hours of drumming up business.

Struggling to keep my business afloat in a tanking economy was doubly hard after gaining custody of my sweet, aging golden retriever who, I learned, howled for hours when left alone. Dog sitters were far beyond my budget, which meant that Porter was often curled under my desk or a back-seat passenger, calm but covering my suits with fuzzy blond fur. Not normally a worrier, I found myself obsessing over how I'd cover my bills.

The unexpected, sparkling background to these uncertain days was that, at age fifty, I had met Pierre. Escaping our lonely marriages by delving into the Internet, we had each fallen upon the fascinating virtual world called Second Life. Looking back, I snicker at fifty-year-olds playing with cartoon avatars, yet the memory of that first typed conversation with the man behind his dancing character remains so vivid. We became easy, nearly instant friends. Months later, as my marriage came to its sad conclusion, I began to admit that what I felt for Pierre was far more than friendship. Over the previous few months he had revealed himself to be the partner I'd been longing for: responsible, funny, and an eager communicator. There was one major glitch. He lived 3,000 miles away on the northern side of a very real border.

My eyes snapped open as last evening's conversation drifted up to consciousness. After a few occasional, exciting, but always too-brief visits and his persistent – though futile – job search around the Pacific Northwest, Pierre had asked a question I had not even dared to ask myself. Would I consider moving out east, rather than him moving west? There was a long silence as we'd stared at each other on our respective video screens. We could be together full time... soon, rather than someday.

Recalling that conversation, I felt the blood pounding in my ears. I might be moving to Canada! Giving up any hope of returning to sleep, I crawled out of bed and into my robe and headed for the kitchen to make a cup of tea. Our words came back in a rush and, on their heels, a surge of tangled feelings.

"It would mean leaving all of your friends and family," he had said, articulating my barely considered thoughts, "and closing down your business. Am I asking too much?" Together we sorted through our first reactions, touched on possibilities, changed the subject, and then circled back to it for hours. We were both risk-takers, enjoying new adventures, so the thought of my moving to Ottawa wasn't really frightening. It was just complex. I began to imagine my friends' and family's reactions. Bad enough that we'd met online. Now I was just going to pack up and move out of the U.S. to live with a man I barely knew? Maybe *we* weren't afraid, but *they* would be.

While our initial in-person meeting and most of our visits since had taken place in Seattle, I had flown to Ottawa a couple of months before to see Pierre in his home city. Friends had warned me about the extreme weather and, since I'd spent some time in upstate New York just a few hours south, I understood their concern.

What I found on my visit though was a city as green as Seattle peppered with neon, lush parks every few blocks, as if the city planners truly appreciated the value of nature. Arched through the suburbs was a thick band of woods and hiking trails, a nearly 14,000-acre greenbelt, filled with a fascinating blend of hard- and softwoods that, thus far, had resisted development. There were two wide, meandering rivers, the Ottawa and the Rideau, and the path-lined Rideau Canal, populated by runners, skaters, and cyclists. All this water helped my seaside eyes relax as I gazed into their grey-green depths. Lebanese, Danish, and Korean groceries; shawarma, Thai, and Mexican restaurants; the constant blend of French and English conversations; all illustrated the variety of cultures that made their home in Ottawa.

Pierre had taken me on long walking and driving tours, showing me the neighbourhoods where he had grown up, smiling as I gawked at turn-of-the-century stone and brick architecture. I marveled at the huge embassies, proudly flying their countries' flags, with smartly-dressed diplomats of every skin-tone climbing in and out of black limousines parked at their curbs. The federal Parliament buildings overlooked a giant green courtyard and were backed by the Ottawa River, conveniently acting as the Ontario-Quebec border. When we crossed the bridge, Pierre spoke his native French, conversing with clerks and waiters, graciously translating their musical exchanges for me.

The highlight of the trip had been riding in his race car at Shannonville Motorsport Park. He had told me about his passion for racing in one of our first typed conversations, a tantalizing fact that I'd been yearning to see. Physically being there, watching him zip around the track and then pulling off his helmet after a dozen laps, his hair curly with sweat, his smile beaming, was even better than I had imagined. When he asked if I would like a ride, I leaped off the pit wall and donned the extra helmet. Shrieking with delight, I lasted five laps around before my stomach had had enough.

"We may have to put you through the Driver's Development Training," he laughed, as we pulled back into the pit. "You won't have motion sickness holding onto the wheel."

"Sign me up!" was my response. Although we teased about it then, I had no idea what that reality might look like. Until last night – months later – I had never considered what it might be like to actually live there.

When the teapot whistled, Porter realized I was up. He ambled out of the bedroom, sniffed hopefully at his food bowl, and gave a long, creaky stretch before circling and resettling at my feet, his back resting below my favourite spot on the couch.

He'd done remarkably well a couple of months earlier, moving from the farm to my small apartment in the city. "We'll head over to the park as soon as the rain has stopped, bud." I pulled my favorite mug from the drainboard, poured hot water over a teabag and added a trickle of milk. "Meanwhile," I said, walking back from the kitchen and resting my mug on the coffee table, "how would you feel about becoming a Canadian dog?"

He answered with a half-hearted *thump thump* of his tail against the beige carpet. It suddenly occurred to me that he might have to go through quarantine if we moved. I couldn't do that to this sweet old boy.

Looking up from him, I gazed around the cozy living room of the condo Pierre and I had hoped would be our first home. Most of the furniture my former husband and I had bought had stayed with him in the country. The pieces around me now were mostly antiques passed down from my parents and Gramps and Gran: Mom's old Singer treadmill sewing machine, the coffee table filled with memories of playing TV Bingo, and Gramps' reupholstered rocker and its ottoman, still acting as a secret toy-chest for a fourth generation of visiting children. How would I get all of this to Ontario?

Moving would mean so many things. In addition to all of the steps it would require, there would be grief... giving up the dream of sharing life in Seattle with Pierre, the dreaded packing of my belongings yet again, saying goodbye to precious people, and once more building a community and support system from scratch. On top of all of that, it would mean breaking my lease, something I had never done before. It seemed such an irresponsible act, and could have long-lasting, if not expensive results.

And what of my business? Over the past six years I had built a clientele of friends and acquaintances, a network of people, many of whom I hoped were beginning to think of me as their Realtor® for Life. Could I just walk away from them and my colleagues, friends, and family? Where was my credibility? Would any these friendships survive?

The biggest question I grappled with, though, as I sipped that middle of the night mug of Sleepytime tea, was *Who would I be in Ottawa?* If I moved across the border, I would not be allowed to work, at least not until the government said so. Having been a proud American – self-employed, thank-you-very-much – most of my adult life, I had no idea how *not* to work. Pierre assured me that we would save money by not having the cross-country visits, even if I never worked again. While the prospect of moving didn't scare me, that thought certainly did. I'd never labeled myself a staunch feminist, but my internal voice was not saying *housewife* or *kept woman* in pleased, self-respecting tones.

But we would be together.

Sipping the last of my tea, looking out my second-story windows at the dripping, green cedar trees, I wondered what the next few weeks would bring. We'd come to only two solid conclusions at the end of the prior night's call: we would spend Christmas together the following month, and there was much to discuss.

Chapter 2

December 2008   One month later

For more than a week, the only people who had left the condo complex were those who had tracked down and donned rarely-used snow boots. Unused to icy surfaces, they hiked their way out with stiff backs and flat-footed steps. The novelty of "snow days" had long worn thin as kids and adults, unable to travel to school or work, grew snappy with cabin fever. Every year we anticipated one or two snowfalls, at least one of which exceeded three inches, enough to keep the wisest commuters home, avoiding the sloped roads and inexperienced winter drivers. Because it was rarely necessary, the city was woefully short on snow-removal equipment. Luckily, mild temperatures usually melted the snowfall within a day or two. But over this past week Seattle had made the national news as cars driven by rash drivers slid down residential hills and plowed into other vehicles and buildings. Two days before, a bus had nearly breached a cement retaining wall and dropped a full load of screaming passengers onto the freeway. For the first time in local memory, the city was covered with a thick sheet of ice, slush, and snow, and Christmas was only two days away.

After a fitful night of sleep, I was up, red-eyed, at the far-too-early hour of 5:30 AM. Pierre was due at Seattle-Tacoma airport late afternoon, but with flights delayed yesterday in Ottawa and dozens canceled in Seattle, we had no idea whether his plane would even be leaving Canada, let alone touching down here.

Having woken me as he left his house for the airport an hour before, whispering goodbye on Skype, he had then called to let me know of their first delay just minutes before I climbed out of bed.

He was at his standing-room-only gate, where airport personnel struggled to maintain a semblance of Christmas spirit. Along with thousands of other would-be passengers, he watched the storm outside and the TV monitors endlessly repeating international weather reports. He promised to update me as soon as anything changed. Vancouver, BC was Pierre's first stop and, at this point anyway, that airport was running on schedule.

We had worked out a grand plan for this holiday. I was to pick him up at SeaTac with Porter and my weekend bag packed, ready to go. From there, we would drive the four hours across the Cascade Mountains to spend a few days with my family in the arid Columbia Basin of Eastern Washington. Moses Lake had grown significantly since my high school days, but it retained its same small-town feel, so very different from the damp, urban tangle of freeways and crowded neighbourhoods that I called home. I would get to share our holiday traditions with my dear Pierre for the first time.

The highlight would be our Christmas Eve fish-fry dinner. I could almost smell hot peanut oil and hear the kitchen banter of we four women preparing this traditional meal. The main dish was provided by Dad who had caught, filleted, and frozen his catches over the previous summer. Dad loved the serenity of fishing, but perhaps equally, his blue eyes would sparkle with an inner delight as we all snuck a morsel or two before the meal, and then polished off every last golden piece of perch, bass, and walleye. After dinner, my nephew and his boys would don their Santa's Helper hats, passing out the presents, and we would open them one at a time, savouring each person's goodies as they were revealed. My grandnephews, at three and five, were the perfect age for tearing into their gifts from Santa Claus. I was certain Pierre would enjoy every moment of it. When we returned to Seattle, we would have one last romantic day tucked into our condo before he had to fly back, and the missing would begin again.

Setting up my laptop on the dining room table, I learned that snow was falling heavily in the mountains. If skiers could get up to Snoqualmie, they would be ecstatic, cutting turns through waist-deep powder. However, cars without chains were being turned back to the city. Web cameras showed bumper-to-bumper traffic and swirls of near whiteout conditions. If it continued, the pass would most likely be closed by noon, and our hopes of being with the family would be quashed. I swallowed the lump in my throat and checked SeaTac Airport's website. The plows and de-icers were having trouble maintaining traction on the runways. While it wasn't closed, many flights were being redirected or delayed. If Pierre finally got out of Ottawa, I wondered how close to Seattle his plane could land.

Looking out the bedroom window, the slate blue of my Volkswagen Passat barely peeked out from under a deep blanket of fresh snow. It looked cozy tucked into its parking spot at the bottom of our sloped lot. Perhaps, if I got it rocking, my all-weather tires could pack and grip the new snow enough to let me make it to the closest plowed road. That thoroughfare – almost a mile of ice away – led directly to Interstate 5 and north to Vancouver. The freeway was bound to be cleared. A million thoughts raced through my mind. If I could make it to Vancouver, if Pierre could get there, *and* if we could find a place to stay, we could at least be together.

First things first. Opening my email, I shot off a quick request to my prayer group.

From: Patrice Elston
Date: Tue, Dec 23, 2008 6:30 AM
To: CSL Connection Circle
Subject: Emergency request from Patrice

Dear *Seattle Center for Spiritual Living* Connection Circle
partners,

Sending you all extra holiday prayers for this crazy week
of weather. If you have travel plans, I hope you are able
to get out and be with your loved ones, or they are able
to get to you.

As you know, Pierre and I made plans to spend this
Christmas together, and we're hitting some (very literal)
roadblocks. Would you mind visualizing this for us?
Happy to do the same for you and yours.

Blessings all around,
Patrice

I sat back for a few moments in prayer, slowing my
breathing and picturing each of the seven online friends
in our group surrounded by their friends and families,
sharing love and the gifts of the season. "This or

something better; Thank you, God. And so it is." I whispered, feeling the serenity of the practice seep through me, as it always did.

Donning my warmest clothes, I tramped out to the parking lot, Porter leading the way. The snow atop the slippery surface was about as *un*-Seattle-like as it could be. Light and powdery, it would be ideal for skiing, but impossible for building a snowman. As hard as I tried, I couldn't tamp a solid footprint into it.

Porter, his puppy-side surfacing in the snow, bounded around the parking lot, sliding and scrambling. Crunching through the layers of ice and snow at the edge, he found the perfect spot, squatted, and melted a yellow puddle into the pristine whiteness. I threw a few handfuls of powder, laughing as he snapped at the air, and then tucked him back inside the condo, promising to rejoin him very soon. *Oh lord,* I thought, *if I have to go up to Vancouver, what will I do with Porter?*

Brushing off just enough snow to gain entry, I slipped into the car's icy interior and cranked over the engine. At least my battery was still doing its job. Gaining traction was going to be unlikely, but I had to try. A moment later it became clear that I needn't have bothered. Once the tires cracked loose of their icy troughs, even the lightest pressure on the gas pedal set them spinning in their tracks.

Bundling back into the condo, I put on the kettle, fed the pup, and checked my phone and email. No messages from Pierre.

As the tea brewed, I began making notes. It was still possible that SeaTac would remain open and Pierre's flight could make it here. From the airport, a taxi ride would cost nearly $100, but he could catch a bus downtown and, with a few transfers, make it to within just under a mile of the condo. It wouldn't be fun or comfortable, but it *was* doable, and he could hike the final route. It was also still possible that the mountain pass would remain open. However, according to the weather reports, the likelihood that the parking lot would melt off enough for us to get the car out over the next day or two was very low. We *might* be able to catch a bus across the mountains, but it would be an all-day trip... if there were even seats available. It was beginning to look as though Christmas with the family wasn't going to happen.

A little over an hour later Pierre called. Their flight had finally been called for boarding. As he and the other west-bound passengers peered out the windows in Ottawa, the de-icing trucks sprayed the fuselage and wings of their aircraft with a thick, white chemical fog. Outside my windows it had begun to snow again just minutes before, and the news had come through. Seattle-Tacoma International Airport was officially closed. Our options were narrowing. If Pierre boarded his flight, it would be a full commitment. Either I had to find a way to get up to Vancouver, or Pierre would have to get down here via rail or bus. Otherwise, we would spend Christmas apart. Neither of us was willing to give up yet. As he took his place in the queue, we weighed the possibility that he might be throwing away a $700 flight across the country and prayed that he wouldn't be heading back on the next possible flight. In the end, we decided that getting on the plane was the only true option, and we said our farewells as he did just that.

I spent the next hour on hold with the Vancouver bus and train ticket offices, sipping cold tea and trying to tune out the Muzak. Eventually, the clerk droned information that no one wanted to hear. Because SeaTac Airport was closed, all other public transportation seats heading south from Vancouver to Seattle were filled. Standby lists were in the double digits.

Crossing another option off the rapidly-dwindling list, I scrutinized the remaining possibilities, looked up another number, tried to stretch away some of the tightness in my back, and dialed again.

After another extended wait on hold, during which I paced from room to room, I was able to get through to an agent at the downtown bus terminal. With a gusty sigh he let me know that there were a few available seats on the last afternoon northbound bus. If I could get into the city in time, I could be on it. Fingers crossed and palms sweating, I dug out my credit card and reserved a ticket.

Throughout the morning, I'd been picturing my beautiful timeshare condominium in downtown Vancouver. Calling the reservation line, I was given a choice to leave a message or stay on hold, "Your approximate wait time will be 18 minutes." My breathless recorded message made it clear that a quick return call would be appreciated. Thinking of the typically long reservation wait-lists for the condos, I tried to stifle the Doubting Thomas in my head imagining *"You want a last-minute unit at Christmas? You're kidding, right?"* Since knowing that response was a real possibility, I pulled up Travelocity and began looking for hotel availabilities.

As I hung up from the next call – a tear-filled, good-luck, hope-to-see-you-soon conversation with my family – the phone buzzed in my hand. Curiously, the readout showed Pierre's number. "Hey sweetie. I thought you were in the air," I answered.

"Yeah. Well." His echoing voice sounded strained, his hand obviously cupped around the mouthpiece. "We all thought we would be, too. We've been sitting here on the tarmac for the past hour, waiting to be cleared for take-off. The captain just let us know it would be at least another forty-five minutes until we're up. We have to stay on this jammed plane, but they let us use our phones for awhile. What have you learned?"

I filled him in on my last few calls, and we talked about options for Porter and our lodging in Vancouver. "I wish I could help you make this all happen, you know," he said softly into his phone.

"I do know, and I appreciate the thought," I said. "Next time, it's your turn. For now, just relax and have a safe flight."

The next two hours were filled with call after call to Vancouver hotels. I worked my way through the list of three- and then budget-stretching four-star places. Every single one was completely booked. The knot in my stomach continued to grow. At last, the call I'd been hoping for came through.

"Believe it or not," the timeshare agent began, "with this weather, we have had a number of cancelations this morning, and the waitlist is empty. You may have to move to a different unit each day, but there is space available for the next three nights." My eyes filled with tears. We were in!

After a quick lunch, I dumped the contents of my huge suitcase onto the bed and repacked the necessities into my backpack. I had the Metro bus schedule tucked deep into my pocket with coins for the rides into the city. It had been a dozen years since I had ridden a city bus, and I prayed that I had read the schedules correctly. There was no way to tell whether any of them would be running in this weather, let alone what their timing would be.

Wrapping Porter in his doggy jacket and boots and bundling into my own, I clipped on his lead, grabbed his bag, rolled-up bed and my backpack, and we slipped and slogged the mile and a half to our friend, Jan's house. I dug her hidden key out from under an indistinguishable lump in the snow that I knew to be a goofy lawn gnome. Laughing at the bouncing reunion between Porter and Jan's three goldens, I tucked his supplies and a big box of chocolate for Jan out of reach atop the fridge. I left her an effusive thank-you note for her last-minute "*Of course you can leave him here*" response to my earlier call, kissed my buddy goodbye on his soft white snout, and hiked out to the first bus stop.

The next three hours were a bus rider's nightmare and reminded me once again of why I was so grateful to own a car. As I waited at the crowded, frozen stop between the first and second leg of the route, the phone again buzzed in my jacket pocket. Tucking it into my hood, Pierre's strained, exhausted-sounding voice told me that the pilot had just made the announcement –

nearly six hours after their scheduled departure—they were next in line for take-off.

Two diesel-reeking, freezing, jerky, standing-smashed-together rides later, my Metro route ended at another bus depot, seven minutes before the coach to Vancouver was due to leave. Squeezing off the bus, and then frantically explaining to the people at the front of the long ticket line why I needed to cut in, I snatched my reserved ticket from under the thick glass window and delivered it to the driver just as he was starting to close the bus door. Settling into the neon blue, disinfectant-smelling seat, I allowed myself the first full breath of the day. We had made it happen. Unless one of our vehicles crashed in the next few hours, we would be together for Christmas.

Chapter 3

December 2008

Moments later, pulling away from the station, I found that the seat beside me, and in fact, most of the seats were empty. After being surrounded by constant chatter and complaints on the previous three rides, the silence was almost eerie. The crunch and slosh of tires through mucky city streets was the only sound. I wondered how many stops there would be on the way to Vancouver, how many north-travelling people we would scoop up – I'd been told, after all, that there were only a few seats remaining – and how long this normally three-hour trip would take.

Gazing at the side of the driver's face a few seats ahead, I became keenly aware of a throbbing ache in my neck. Reaching up, I dug my fingertips into the muscles, loosening the banded fibres, massaging fresh blood into my shoulders. I couldn't remember a day so filled with tense worry and seat-of-my-trousers decision making. Looking out the window, my messy-haired reflection smiled back, and I thought, *all of that work paid off!* As we slowly accelerated onto the slushy freeway, a sense of relief flooded up my neck and across my shoulders, and I let my memories flow.

Snowflakes swirled past the window as I recalled Pierre and my first in-person meeting. Fewer than a handful of my friends had encouraged that step. All of the others thought I was taking a huge risk. They were right; people played all kinds of games in the virtual world. Some pretended to be young, sexy, and wildly successful. Many men and women played roles designed to entice or tease, neglecting to recall – or not caring – that behind each dancing, flying, and teleporting cartoon character was a real person with a fragile heart.

Even though none had ever met Pierre, they couldn't believe he was the man he portrayed himself to be online, but I knew. We had often talked from evening far into the early morning hours. I felt as though I'd found a rare gem. Not only did he dive deep with me, sharing his observations and beliefs, but he seemed to really love doing so. Superficiality and game-playing were as foreign and distasteful to him as they were to me. Not all our conversations were serious; I often laughed aloud at his goofy, off-the-cuff remarks and to my surprise, he laughed at mine. The truly refreshing part about his humour, though, was that it was *never* cruel or crass. He was real, alright... and extremely kind. His curiosity about my perspective on everything from gardening to spirituality and politics flattered, but what most impressed me was his willingness to listen carefully. Even though we exposed a few of our emotional warts and scars in those first months of online chatting, he never showed a single sign of running away. For the first time in my life, I thought as I anticipated that first face-to-face meeting, I might meet my match.

Our first encounter happened purely by chance, if you believe in chance. Our cartoon avatars had met in a virtual blues club in Second Life – a program some referred to as *The Sims* on steroids. The club and our characters were all pixels; everything from the bar to the glitter-ball, including every dancing couple we could see on our computer screens, had been created by programmers and designers. The entire world, in fact, was built by people who visited the site. Someone had even designed pink and blue *pose-balls:* spots strategically placed around the dance floor that when clicked on, automatically stepped, spun, and twirled our avatars into perfectly-synchronized dancing partners.

One character stood alone on a tiny raised stage behind a moving stereo turntable. The blues tunes playing through our speakers or in our headsets came from the digital library of that DJ avatar – the man controlling it sitting in his home office in Florida, clicking through his iTunes library, choosing a perfect playlist for an audience that spanned the globe.

I had been swing dancing with a fellow who had teleported me in to the place, a mortgage broker from east Texas. The Instant Message box on my screen had been gushing with his self-important monologue, enumerating the many complex loans he had secured for clients over the previous months. For the third time I typed, "Um, Broker? Did you hear me request that we discuss anything but work? I come to SL to get away from RL [real life]." For the first time since we had met three-quarters of an hour before, his typing stopped. The next thing I knew, my avatar was frozen in a bizarre position, and he was gone, having either logged off or teleported away. Sighing with relief, I clicked off the pose-ball and my perpetually 23-year-old blond avatar stood awkwardly alone on the dance floor for a few moments, as I scanned the room with my arrow keys. I took in the design – blue lighting and giant posters of BB King and Stevie Ray Vaughn – until my eye was caught by a single gent kicked back on a bar stool. His avatar was looking directly at me, so I clicked to read his profile. He'd called himself Kam Larsson. His profile was sparse. Just a few notes about being inworld to learn, and three magic words: *drama-free zone*. I clicked to send him an Instant Message just as one popped open on my screen.

Kam Larsson: Hello. Looks like your dance partner left.

Patrice Fisseaux: Yes. Best thing that's happened all day. ☺

Kam Larsson: LOL! [pause] Do you speak French?

Patrice Fisseaux: Unfortunately, not. Beautiful language, though. Do you?

Kam Larsson: It's actually my first language.

Patrice Fisseaux: Wonderful! Are you in France?

Kam Larsson: No. Canada.

Patrice Fisseaux: Ah! I'm a big fan of Canada.

Kam Larsson: ☺ Would you like to dance?

And I said yes.

Within a couple of weeks of after-dinner typed-out chats, the two of us found in each other sensitive, genuine people, and our hesitation about exploring each other's minds went by the wayside. There was no body language, no intonation, and no prejudice to overcome. All we had was a connection of mind, carefully chosen words, and the flow of ideas that revealed dreams, doubts, and the longings of our unfulfilled lives. As the weeks went on, our friendship deepened, and conversations lasted later into the night.

We exchanged photographs, his first one a funny shot next to his car, his head encased in a full-face helmet, mine a black and white of me at age six. When we finally dared to reveal our present-day faces, we planned it out, pressing the e-mail Send buttons at the same moment. Opening his message from my inbox, I stared at the attached file, letting my mouse hover over it for long minutes, afraid to open it, anxious that the man I had begun to care about might somehow repulse me. I could hear the occasional soft *bling*s of his comments arriving in our Second Life chat box on the screen behind my e-mail. *Oh my god. What was he saying? Which should I look at first?* Eventually, curiosity about his appearance won out, and I opened his photo file. A handsome, dark-haired gentleman with Roman statue features smiled out at me. With a flood of relief and magnetism, I quickly minimized the email screen and scrolled back through his prior few messages.

Kam Larsson: OMG. ***You're beautiful!!***

Kam Larsson: Patrice? Are you there? Did you get my picture?

Kam Larsson: Wow. I had a feeling you would look like this. That little girl you first sent me… she is still here in this photo. Gorgeous. Playful.

Kam Larsson: Hello?

Keys clicking, I hurriedly typed.

Patrice Fisseaux: Sorry. I'm here. ☺ Thank you for your kind comments. ☺ It took a while to screw up the courage to open yours. Would you like to know what I think of it?

Kam Larsson: YES!!! Tease!!!

So, grinning at our on-screen avatars sitting around a beach campfire, I told him.

Weeks later, when Second Life integrated voice chat into the program, we graduated to audio, where I learned that he had a smoldering bass voice. Surprisingly, I heard no trace of a French accent. When I expressed my slight disappointment at that, he switched seamlessly to French, telling me with a joking flair, that he did, indeed, speak the language, and very well thank you very much! We laughed through his translation.

Once we began talking, we were no longer limited by the speed of our typing, but neither could we hit a backspace key to edit our words. Despite that, conversation flowed easily with few misunderstandings and easy clarifications. Before long, Pierre dug out and plugged in an old web camera and, as easy as that, I was watching him chat. My shyness at being on camera kept me from purchasing a webcam, but when I replaced the ancient desktop computer, its laptop successor's built-in camera urged my hand. As with each of the steps before it, my initial bashfulness was short-lived.

Neither of us could remember who first suggested a real-life meeting; it was probably me. I wasn't interested in an online romance. Our conversations had deepened to a place where I finally admitted—weeks after he had—that my feelings for him had far surpassed friendship. But could that translate from the screen to reality? Would I be attracted or repelled by his scent, his habits—and he, by mine? Could our connection transcend the brain-mate status we had created into the physical world of passion, joy, laundry, and groceries? Only meeting in the real world would tell, so we made it happen.

Palms sweating, heart pounding, I paced SeaTac airport's long, people-packed baggage claim area from end to end three times, willing the clock to move faster, and jumping when his flight number on the arrival board finally switched from *On Time* to *Arrived*. Tucking the finger-dampened *Seattle Met* magazine back into its rack with shaking hands, I waited at the top of the escalator with a trying-not-to-be-nervous smile and watched as – what felt like a million minutes later – he ascended from the international gates.

His face was open-hearted, warm, and then briefly puzzled and distressed as I reached my hand toward him while backing away. *Come,* I beckoned, leading him to a private place around a corner to a tucked-in spot under the escalator. Letting his bag and my purse tumble around our feet, we slid into each other's arms, fitting together flawlessly, breathing in each other's scents. His was a heady mix of his warm, smooth skin, a light spice and a slight hint of mint. Seconds later I learned that he had just brushed his teeth—a thoughtful gesture that I wished I had considered. But swept into that first minutes-long kiss, every other thought disappeared.

When we finally broke apart and my mind began to work again, the first question that floated up was, *Oh. My. God! Is this real?* The delighted smile on his face made it clear that he, too, had felt those breathtaking fireworks. Gathering up our belongings, we slowly moved through the airport and out to the car, grinning like explorers who had just discovered hidden treasure. We held hands, first one leading, then the other, as we tore our eyes from each other to watch where we were going. Touching him, seeing him in person didn't compare to video. *So, this is what the love of my life looks like,* I thought, soaking in his gait, his broad chest and shoulders, his stocky, solid body moving next to me. It was the beginning of an incredible time of visits, culminating with this one… our first official holiday together.

Ascending from my reverie, I found that the bus was at a standstill next to a bland yellow brick building. A dozen new passengers were trudging from a terminal through freezing rain, stowing luggage, and queueing up to come aboard. Looking out at the signs, I realized we were already in Everett, almost a third of the way to the border. Across the aisle, a woman a few years my junior slid into the seat and dropped her Boeing-logoed duffle bag into the window seat beside her. Our eyes met briefly as she shivered and draped her dripping jacket over the turquoise seat in front of her bag. She smiled, saying, "Nice that they provide drying racks, isn't it?" Grinning back, I reached across the seats to introduce myself. I learned that her name was Lisa, and she was on her way to Whistler to spend the holidays skiing with her kids. "How about you?" she asked, opening a Thermos of steaming mint tea and filling two paper cups. "Going home for Christmas?" I gratefully accepted the proffered cup and began to tell her my story.

Chapter 4

December 2008

Gabbing through the stops at Mount Vernon and Bellingham, Lisa and I barely noticed the next couple of hours. As the bus filled with passengers, Lisa scooted her jacket and bag under the seat next to mine and slid in beside me. We shared our stories easily, as complete strangers sometimes do. Whatever the reason, we transformed what might otherwise have been a boring, uncomfortable ride together into a getting-to-know-you adventure.

"... so that is our crazy 21st century love story," I finished, as signs announcing duty-free stores flashed by. I laughed with her at the bizarre odds of Pierre and my meeting online. "Now, we've begun to consider my moving to Ottawa. Of course, I have a million different feelings about that, not to mention knowing *nothing* about immigration."

"You're talkin' to the right lady!" she said, giving my forearm a gentle bump with her elbow. "My son just went through that over the past year or so.... Unfortunately for me, it means my first grandbaby is gonna grow up across the border, but Vancouver's not so far. Unless those Canadian girls have speedy deliveries, I should be able to be there just a few hours after getting the call." Her eyebrows danced in anticipation. We toasted with the last cups of her tea to the upcoming event. "I'm worried about her up on the mountain this weekend, but she's been skiing Whistler and Blackcomb since she was five years old, and nobody's gonna tell her to stay off the slopes. Reminds me a lot of her husband, that one," she smiled. "So... What do you want to know about moving up to Canada?"

"Well...," I stumbled, not really knowing what questions to ask. "Is your son a Canadian citizen now?"

Lisa's deep guffaw rolled out over the heads of our fellow passengers. "That's his eventual goal, yeah. Turns out it's not enough to be married to a Canadian. He found out that there are lots of steps he's gotta take before he'll become a citizen. In order for him to stay, the government requires that he either work at a particular job or be in school. So right now, he's getting his Master's degree in something called Geophysics at UBC. He's got a student visa, which lets him stay up there for two years, and next will apply for his Permanent Resident Card – basically the same as our Green Card. Should be another couple of years before that comes through...."

Interrupting, the bus driver's voice crackled through the overhead intercom, "Ladies and gentlemen, our next stop is the Peace Arch Border Crossing into British Columbia. Please be certain you have filled out and signed your Customs Declaration Card and have it and your passport out and ready to present upon arrival. You will be required to carry all of your belongings into the customs office. Border officers have the right to open and inspect any bags. Unless there is a serious problem, we should be re-loaded and back on our way to Vancouver in approximately forty-five minutes. Thank you for your attention." His drone made it obvious that it wasn't the first time he had made that speech. Around us the murmurs died down as we dug through purses and bags, balanced books and briefcases on our laps and filled in or re-checked our forms.

Climbing down from the bus and clumsily pushing through the glass door, I shifted my backpack further onto my shoulder. My fidgeting fingers gripped the required paperwork as I advanced toward the stern-faced woman at the narrow podium. *Why?* I thought. *Why does this border crossing ritual always make me so nervous? I have nothing to hide. I've done nothing wrong.* Rationalization aside, my heart pounded as I watched her grill the people ahead and either direct them to an open door or to a long counter on the far side of the room.

Unsmiling agents roughly zipped open luggage and rifled through personal belongings. They asked questions in voices too low to make out. Three passengers stood at that counter attempting to shield their laid-bare underclothes from the rest of us. Embarrassed, we couldn't help but watch, concerned that our bags too might be scrutinized.

And then, "*Next.*" Her lips were thin and pinched. Small, pale eyes squinted through severe, black-framed glasses. The questions were the usual ones: Why are you coming to Canada? What is your final destination? How long are you staying? Are you bringing any firearms with you? I knew to be clear and brief. I'm meeting my boyfriend for Christmas; My timeshare in Vancouver; For three days; No weapons. Carefully inspecting my passport and declaration form, she scowled, looking deep into my eyes, searching for hesitation or anything in my demeanor that indicated deception or fear.

Unexpectedly, her already-rigid back straightening even further, she asked, "Your boyfriend is not from Vancouver? Where is he coming from?" When I told her, she barked, "And you're not going back to Ottawa with him?"

My voice caught in my throat. "No. I'm returning to Seattle... to work. I... I have a round-trip ticket." Fumbling in my purse, I pulled the printed stub into view.

Her eyes narrowed further as she stood ram-rod straight in silence. I drew in a deep breath and looked up at her, hearing my pulse pound in my ears, refusing to be baited into babbling. She cleared her throat, waited another long moment, finally stamped my passport and handed it back. Her head-jerk toward the door was the only indication that I was free to exit and re-board the bus. Hefting my pack and slipping away from her probing glower, I glanced back and sent well-wishes to the still-waiting passengers in line. *What an unhappy woman,* I thought, shaking the last of the nervousness from my shoulders.

Lisa smiled up as I tucked back into the window seat. "Where do they *find* those people?" she asked, tucking her book away.

"So, your border officer was also less than welcoming?" I asked.

"Yeah. It's typical, though," she said. "Some days you get lucky, but mostly, the folks who want the job aren't really the friendly type."

I asked whether crossing the border was any easier for her son now that he was married to a Canadian and had a student visa.

"Well, you'd think so. The sad thing is, right there on his student permit it says it doesn't guarantee re-admittance to Canada, so he's still just as stressed out at the border after he visits us. We hope it will be easier once his Permanent Residency comes through."

Huge Canadian and American flags ruffled in the breeze beside the immigration station. An hour and a half after arriving, the last slump passenger climbed back aboard. There was a smattering of applause as the bus fired up and we continued onto the freeway.

The final leg of our journey was much quieter, each of us contemplating our upcoming visits. As we wound through Vancouver's city streets, Lisa pulled the rubber band off a tattered address book in her purse and thumbed through it. Jotting on the back of a grocery receipt, she handed me two names and numbers, another woman's and her own. She explained that her son had been referred to this immigration attorney, and she had given him some great advice. "Maybe she can help you, too, if you do decide to move up here. And..." she said, glancing away almost shyly, "you're always welcome to stop in for a gab if you come up to Everett if you stay."

Hugging her goodbye in front of Vancouver's brightly lit station, I thanked her for her gracious company and wished her a safe and fun weekend with her kids. I hoped to see her again but was unsure what the next few months would bring. Watching as she was swept up into the exuberant arms of a laughing, obviously-expecting couple who had hopped out of a mini-van, I chucked my backpack onto the seat of a cab.

Half an hour later, after a quick stop at an all-night grocery, I unloaded clothes into the dresser of the timeshare condo. The clock radio beside the bed read 11:30. Nineteen floors above the still-moving city, I sat in a floor-to-ceiling-windowed breakfast-nook, waiting in perfect stillness. Catching glimpses of Stanley Park's blackness and glints of Vancouver Harbour through a forest of green glass high-rises, I wondered, *When will he get here?* In the quiet, my very empty stomach rumbled, prompting contemplation of today's horrible eating schedule. *I hope they fed Pierre on the plane,* I thought, *even if it was just airline food.*

I rose to switch on the gas fireplace, then sliced an almost mealy apple and some sharp cheddar cheese onto a plate. Just as I tucked back into my nook seat, the telephone on the kitchen wall rang, and I jumped, flinging an apple wedge two feet in the air.

"Good evening, this is the front desk calling. Sorry to bother you, but a gentleman has arrived asking for you. Would you like to speak to him?" Moments later Pierre was at the door and then was in my arms.

Patrice Lefebvre

Chapter 5

December 2008

❝We really ought to go out at some point today to find something to eat," I said, grinning and brushing crumbs onto the floor. Lunchtime had come and gone with only some chips and salsa to sustain us, and our stomachs were rumbling like some silly, discordant choir.

His gentle smile from the pillow next to me agreed, yet neither of us moved to pull back the covers or untangle our limbs. There was a comfort between us that I had never experienced before. A feeling that here, in this warm, quiet place far above the city, I had found the love I'd been searching for, a healing balm for my saddened soul. His calm independence felt so familiar, yet I also sensed the sincerity of his caring – not only in his words, but in his voice and his touch. It was as though my desire for a true partner was reflected on his face. Talking about every subject that emerged, looking for long minutes into each others' eyes, it seemed we might both be recognizing the answer to our longing. It was mid-afternoon before Pierre's appetite required a meal, and we finally crawled out of bed to explore the city.

"Oh, one last thing," I said, dropping my coat onto the couch before donning it. "I need to send a quick email."

Pierre unzipped his thick jacket and slid down into a chair with a sigh.

From: Patrice Elston
Date: Wed, Dec 24, 2008 2:30 PM
To: CSL Connection Circle
Subject: Thank You!!!

Dear Connection Circle partners,

Prayer works!
Although Pierre and I weren't able to be with my family in eastern WA, we ARE together! Thank you so much for your prayer support.
Looking forward to reading about your Christmas adventures next week.

Blessings, Patrice

I quickly slipped on my boots and jacket and apologized for the delay.

"You know about my CSL group, right?" I said, as we walked a few doors down the hall to the nearly silent elevator.

He nodded.

"Well, yesterday morning I asked for their prayers to help us be together; I wanted to let them know that our prayers had worked."

With a slight tilt of his head, Pierre reminded me of all the work I'd done to get here.

"Yes," I said, smiling as we stepped into the elevator, "but who knows whether all of those inspired ideas and connections would have happened if it hadn't been for them?"

He pulled me into a bear hug in the mirrored space. "You…" he said. And I saw the sparkle in his eyes reflected all around us.

The shopping district of Robson Street was a short walk away. We slogged our way along rough, ice- and slush-covered sidewalks, weaving through crowds of chattering, bundled-up teens and frowning men obviously searching for last-minute Christmas gifts. Suddenly, a familiar scent wafted up the street, transporting me back to Christmas holidays in San Francisco. Half a block ahead, behind a waist-high cart no bigger than a child's desk, stood a stout, bearded gentleman, his neck wrapped securely in a bright green woolen scarf. Five or six brown paper cones were tucked into holes in a board in front of him, and steam escaped from the bin below. "Chestnuts! Get'cher hot roasted chestnuts here!"

"Oh, Pierre! Have you had roasted chestnuts before?" I asked, skipping and tugging him toward the cart. The twinkly-eyed vendor handed over a cone with a little nod. A first for Pierre, he tentatively gave one a try.

"Interesting," he said with a slight grimace, and one more of the oddly-textured treats was plenty for him. As we stood juggling the hot paper from hand to hand, I munched the dense, rich nuts, and a realization occurred to me. Discovering and trying new foods had become a passion over the years. Nearly everyone I knew, family and friends, experimented with, and loved discussing, new and exotic cuisines. It had never crossed my mind that he wouldn't be a foodie, too. I knew Pierre enjoyed sushi – as we were now headed for my favourite Vancouver sushi restaurant. And yet perhaps here it was, our first dissimilarity.

Over a dinner of steaming, salty edamame, the freshest sashimi smelling of the sea, and seaweed-wrapped sushi, our conversation wandered among the differences between my west-coast world and his eastern, French Canadian one. As I listened, he explained that his work required regular contract changes; he seemed to enjoy new beginnings and moving between departments. As he was regularly recruited for new consulting positions, it was clear that his reputation as an intelligent, flexible businessman was solid.

I recalled introducing him to Ethiopian food at our first meeting. There had been no reluctance when I'd suggested it. Rather, it was that he didn't search for or *crave* variety. He *liked* his standard fare: soup and sandwich for lunch; meat with sauce, vegetables, and rice or potatoes at dinner. I couldn't imagine it. In fact, I was pretty certain I'd be bored out of my mind if forced to eat that way. So, I smiled, sighing with relief as his eyes slid closed with ecstasy at his first taste of *unagi* – smoked eel sushi.

That evening back in the condo, we snuggled side-by-side on the rich leather couch in front of a warm gas fireplace, discussing the upcoming months. After a time, I realized that we were no longer talking hypothetically of whether I would move to Ottawa, but rather more in terms of how we were going to make it happen. I told him about Lisa's son's advice from the immigration lawyer and his receiving a two-year student visa.

"It seems they'd only let me stay for a short time as a visitor, and then I'd have to return to the states. The problem – according to Lisa – is that I'd have to be accepted into a college program before the government would issue a student permit."

"Ottawa has some excellent post-secondary schools. Algonquin College, University of Ottawa, Carleton University.... Would you like to go back to school?"

"I've always loved learning," I replied. "But I won't be allowed to work to pay for it. I haven't really considered what I'd like to do next. I'm finding that real estate isn't the best fit for me. And I definitely don't want to go back to running a massage therapy business."

"Fair enough. What have you dreamt about doing? If you could be anything..."

A few quiet minutes passed as I sat thinking. "Well, I've considered becoming a speech therapist, but I have a feeling the science requirements would be beyond me."

He was already searching Ottawa U's website for the program. Together, we explored its pages and my concerns were confirmed. The prerequisites alone would mean taking a few semesters of science courses, and then would come a two-year Master's program that looked intense and not-at-all fun.

"Ok, so, what else?" he asked.

"It's not very practical..." I began, "but I do love to write."

The next hour was rich with discourse as we discussed types of writing, making a living, and how I might handle not working – in fact, being supported – for possibly the next few years. Feeling hot tears in my eyes, it struck me that no one had ever offered me that option. During my university days I'd lived on family and student loans and part-time restaurant wages. It had been hard, and repaying the loans had taken many years of diligent work. Having been self-employed for twenty-five years, the thought of a break was delicious, yet at the same time, the pit in my stomach revealed my apprehension. What would happen to my self-esteem? Who was I if I wasn't a worker? What would it feel like to be a full-time student again, but not only that, *a housewife?*

Pierre listened patiently as I stumbled through expressing my feelings about these variables. The one thought that arose again and again as I grappled with the dilemma was *Are there any other viable options? Is it this or continuing to live apart?* Finally, we put it away for the night, choosing instead to enjoy the present. I had research to do over the next few weeks, but for now, we were together, and it was Christmas.

Patrice Lefebvre

Chapter 6

February 2009   Two months later

"This is really happening." Pierre's sleepy voice reached across the miles into Jan's cozy living room. Propped up against fluffy new pillows, his earnest face filled my screen. His image gently rose and fell as his laptop, perched on his chest, migrated with each breath. His eyelids were beginning to droop, the blinks becoming longer and more labored. We'd been on Skype for two hours, discussing the previous days, those to come, and our dreams of life together. Adding in the three-hour time difference, it wasn't surprising that he was nodding off.

My laptop sat next to me on the hide-a-bed where I lay curled up, stretching my tired lower back. Having to be up early for work in the morning, Jan had tucked into her room two hours before. We shared a good cry before she headed down the hallway, when the looming elephant became almost tangible; it might be months or even years before we would see each other again.

Once Jan's pups fell silent behind her bedroom door, Porter paced from room to room before finally heaving himself up onto the mattress and settling against my feet with a long sigh. Three blinks later and he was asleep. I could relate to his exhaustion, but my mind was unwilling to let me rest.

I spent the previous weeks selling, discarding, giving to friends, and donating unwanted clothes, furniture and various bric-a-brac. Three days ago, a dozen dear friends helped tote almost all my remaining belongings down the steps and into my real estate mentor's rigs. Once the trailer and van were packed, I ordered gourmet pizzas and shared a final meal in the empty Shoreline condo with my loving and generous friends. Eyeballing the small left-over pile sitting in the middle of the cavernous condo, I prayed all of it would fit in my car. If not, I guessed I'd be packing and shipping boxes to Ottawa.

Soon after the last car departed, I once again dried my tears, and my girlfriend Leanne and I drove Daryl's van to Moses Lake. There, with the help of family, we re-packed everything into Gramps' storage garage for what will hopefully be a short stay.

This afternoon, after shampooing the condo carpets, my spatially-talented friend Jenni arrived and helped pack into my Passat all I can take as a visitor to Canada. I doubt even an extra piece of paper could fit into my trunk.

In Ottawa, the new bed that Pierre lay in was delivered and set up around noon. Over the previous week, he had dropped off a couple of patio chairs, his clothes, and a few boxes from his old house. Some were already unpacked, some waited on the chilly wood floor. His voice echoed through the mostly empty space.

Moving forward, he made what was, to him, a very simple decision. He chose to start over afresh, leaving nearly all of his furnishings and their corresponding memories with his ex. In exploring a few furniture websites, we found that our basic decorating tastes were similar, although my family antiques aren't his favourite. They're all relatively simple in design, however, he confessed that he's just not a fan of "old." We will find a balance between antique and his more modern preferences. Something classic, perhaps Craftsman or mission style with those clean lines.... *Simple elegance,* he calls it, and I agree.

"Is the bed comfy?" I asked, propping my head up on my hand and attempting to find the softest spot on the mattress.

"It is," he said. "I think this was a good choice. Bet it's going to be a lot better with you here in it."

"I cannot wait."

It seemed that another great choice was our new apartment. Built on a three-block strip between the canal and the river, it sits in a district called Old Ottawa

South, tellingly referred to as The Golden Triangle by real estate brokers. With such easy proximity to the city core and waterfront, property values are steep.

Having perused photos of a dozen other apartments he'd visited across the city, I felt my breath catch when I saw this one. He emailed the ad the day it was listed and was able to meet the landlord for a showing that afternoon. Sharing additional pictures and his impressions from the apartment's parking lot, we discussed what he had learned. Three generations of the landlord's Romanian family live in the building and seem meticulous about its care. The unit was only available because its former tenant had been evicted for breaking the building's non-smoking rule. Most of the tenants had been there for years. The winter salt was obviously mopped regularly from the lobby floor, and one of his photos showed a roller and a five-gallon bucket of dove grey paint sitting inside the unit's front door. We both agreed that we loved it, so he walked back in and filled out their application. The following day the landlord contacted his referrals, and Pierre was invited back to sign the lease.

Just like that, it was ours.

It's planted on a quiet corner just across the canal from the Glebe, Ottawa's upscale earthy urban district. It is probably the closest we will get to the free-spirited Seattle feeling within the city limits. Pierre's commute, still the north/south route along the parkway, will be less than half of what it has been. Depending on the season, he could even skate to work on the Rideau Canal, which is turned into the famous "world's largest skating rink" in winter, or bicycle along its bordering paths. I haven't skated since high school but loved it then and look forward to joining my hockey-playing gent on the frozen waterway.

Pierre said there are plenty of places to walk with Porter. A couple of blocks away, Saint Paul University has dog-friendly acreage, and he said that judging by the number of people being tugged in that direction, Porter won't be wanting for playmates. Directly across the street from the university are three stores he swears I will love: a bookstore, a health food store, and a five-star-rated vegetarian restaurant, *The Green Door*. "Maybe they do take-out and we can have their sides with our steak or pork chops," he teased.

When I first called tonight, he turned his laptop around and slowly walked me through the space, showing me everything from the entryway through both nearly-bare bedrooms, the tiny, but immaculate bath, walk-through kitchen, and main living areas.

"Beautiful Feng Shui," I told him. "Lots of windows – I'm sure it will have lovely light."

He explained with some trepidation that the smell of the new paint barely covered the underlying tang of the former tenant's cigarettes, so although it is frigid outside, he is leaving a few windows ajar.

It is touching to hear how concerned he is about my move. It seems he struggles to believe that I'm leaving my life behind to be with him, and it sounds as though he's worried that I may find it hard to find like-minded friends. I'm just going to trust that they are there and that we will attract each other. In the meantime, I will have *him* and my online connections.

"This might not be easy, honey," he said more than once. "Not only the immigration thing, but your move from the hippie Northwest to this Catholic government town. I just want to spoil you and give you a happy life."

After a lifetime of living in Ottawa, he was ready to leave what he calls his somewhat-stodgy city. His visits to the west coast had liberated feelings he had long ago lost sight of, but being the man that he is, he would never move without securing solid employment. It would have been great if one of the contracts he applied for in Seattle or Vancouver had panned out... but no. Private industry is a mostly-foreign environment to him these days, and just as in Ontario, those contracts went to local, well-known applicants. While those doors kept closing, Ottawa head-hunters continued to call with government opportunities. So, hopefully, as I live the bright, west-coast, life-affirming values – our values – he will feel freer to laugh and let himself play, regardless of where we live.

Jolting awake with a start, Pierre murmured, "Sweetheart, I need to get some sleep. I've got to be up in less than four hours to get to the airport."

"Of course, my love," I said. "I'll be at SeaTac to pick you up at 11:30."

"I'll check in with you when we're taking off."

"Sweet dreams, mon Pierre. See you very, very soon."

Flipping his screen to his dark screensaver and setting his laptop onto the bed, I heard him burrow down into the covers. Within moments, his breath had deepened into his soft, peaceful snore. Again, I thought, *how I wish I were able to fall asleep so easily.* With that rhythmic background hum, though, it wouldn't be long before I, too, would be dreaming.

Upon his 11:30 AM arrival, we will tuck his backpack into the small reserved space behind his seat and begin six days of driving across the continent. It's good that Pierre is keen to drive because, just as his snoring lulls me to sleep, so too does the steady hum of a car engine.

This will be his first time seeing the northern states. We'll cross six mountain passes, and so far, the weather reports are showing no big storms that would hold us up or hinder our view. The Passat is freshly serviced, and since Porter has never been carsick, the trip *should* be incident-free. Ah, well. Whatever happens, we'll handle it.

As much prayer as I have done, the one thing that still clutches at my stomach is the distant border crossing. I have to admit – and Pierre has, too – I am a bit nervous. The immigration lawyer we called shared some tips and a long list of ridiculous red-tape details. Her best piece of news was that, unlike mine, Porter's immigration will be a snap. No quarantine is required, just a current rabies vaccine and a simple health declaration from our vet.

We did decide to ignore her recommendation of crossing at the Peace Arch in British Columbia. Rather than traverse the more northerly Trans-Canada Highway, we will drive across the States, knowing that we risk being refused entry when crossing from Michigan into Ontario. I planned our trip in careful detail. There are people I want to introduce to Pierre on this journey, and friends or family are more than willing to put us up for three of our nights. We have hotels booked in Bismarck and Lansing, perfect stopping points where neither of us knows a soul.

I am choosing to chant up a helpful person at the border who will grant a six-month visitor's visa and wave us on our way home. It's damned uncomfortable for us control-freaks to be at the mercy of the border officer on duty. Following the lawyer's checklist, we have made certain to have all our paperwork in order, so there shouldn't be a problem. It is, after all, our time to be together.

Chapter 7

February - March 2009

Greeted by Porter's white, heart-shaped face peeking up over the edge of the unfamiliar bed, I slowly shifted onto my other side and reached to wake Pierre. His eyes snapped open and almost immediately softened into a look that brought a warm flush to my cheeks. The rest of my body felt as though it had been stuffed into a can and shaken – repeatedly. I will never understand how long-distance truck drivers do it. Four solid days of driving or riding in my usually comfy car, sleeping on different beds each night, and not knowing what's to come wound me up like a watch-spring twisted a turn too far. Looking over Pierre's pillow-messed hair at the illuminated clock, *ugh, 6:30,* I realized that in a little over two hours the verdict would come. We would get to go home, or I would be turned back. Pulling the covers back up, I heard my stomach give a low rumble.

Our trip began with a repeat of Pierre's Christmas flight delays, although, luckily, this setback only lasted a couple of hours. That extra block of time waiting for his flight to arrive was actually a godsend. I drove out to my old waterfront neighbourhood and favourite city viewpoint, Alki Beach, to breathe in the salt air. Huddled in my warmest jacket, I walked, balancing along the top of the sea-wall, listening to gulls screech as they floated on the icy water. *How long will it be,* I wondered, *until I stand at the edge of the ocean again?* Thinking back on Jan's departure to work that morning brought a fresh stab of grief. The tears on my cheeks hadn't only come from the raw wind off the water.

Knowing it was the last time I would pick up Pierre at the airport, the dark cement buildings, wet from a typical rainy evening, seemed especially gloomy. For the first time, I chose not to meet him as close to his gate as possible. Instead, I joined a funeral-like procession of cars traveling in circles around the perimeter of the parking garage. The lump in my throat persisted as I drove slowly past baggage claim again and again, until, finally, he stepped out the doors into the grey drizzle.

Scooting against him in this tiny Michigan hotel room, I said, "It was sad, wasn't it?"

"Sad? This?" he asked, arching his head back to peer down at me.

"Ah," I smiled, "No. *This* is heavenly. I meant saying goodbye to the airport."

"It was," he said, holding me close. "Our first kiss happened there… as well as some other pretty intense hellos and goodbyes. From here on out, though, we'll fly together. It will be better, don't you think?"

And just like that, my melancholy dissolved; I tilted my chin up and kissed him. Later, watching him slip out of bed and disappear into the tiny bathroom, I recalled our past few days.

Leaving SeaTac behind us, we angled up through the suburbs of Renton and Issaquah and onto eastbound I-90. Snoqualmie Pass, a dazzling zig-zag stretch of highway I'd travelled countless times, was remarkably dry: a black strip of asphalt surrounded by ridge after ridge of snow-laden evergreens. Although I'd had very little sleep and car's hums usually knocked me out, my excitement level kept me wide awake and chatting, even as we dropped from the mountains onto flat, open farmland.

Arriving late at my sister and brother-in-law's shoreline home in Moses Lake, there was only time for a brief visit with them and their kids before everyone retired to bed. Morning brought the sweet sounds of my two grand-nephews' giggles and the heady, magnetizing scents of coffee and bacon. Laughing and chattering through the meal – and avoiding teary eye contact – we promised to be back for a visit as soon as we could. On the way out of town, Pierre and I stopped in at Gramps' Alzheimer's care facility for one last farewell. Hard to know whether Grampsy will remember that I'm moving to Canada; I just pray that I get to see him again.

Our second day of driving was somewhat white-knuckled. Over nine hours on the road, we traversed four winding high-mountain passes in Idaho and Montana. Our luck held. Only Homestake Pass, which I drove us across just after sunset, had a few icy patches.

Arriving in Bozeman around dinnertime, we wound through quiet neighbourhoods to my friends, Diane and Travis' home.

"Puh-treesio!" I heard, as she burst from the doorway.

"Di-hanny!" I called back with a whoop. "Will you take a look at that beautiful round tummy?" Standing under the warm porch light, she and Travis were beaming. After months of tests, injections, and miraculous medical procedures, their first baby was shaping my dear friend into the mother she had dreamt of being. "You are glorious!" I whispered into her ear, hugging her tight. "Congratulations to you both!"

The evening passed more quickly than we thought possible. We shared a meal, and Pierre and Travis talked guitars and cars, as if they'd been pals forever and were not just meeting for the first time.

"Would you be interested in seeing my Packard?" Travis asked as we began clearing the table.

"Your Packard? You have a *Packard? Here?*" was Pierre's response.

"Yep. I've been remodeling it. Of course, at the rate I'm going, it will probably be done about the time I'm too old to drive…" and they disappeared into the garage.

With Porter at our feet, Diane and I attempted to placate their irate tabby, Jed. I'd known Jeddy since he was a sleek orange handful; now at about Porter's age, his once-bouncy body had become lean and stiff. Eventually, he crept onto the back of the sofa and took a light, vigilant nap while Diane and I caught up on three long years of living apart, sharing our excitement at the upcoming changes in our lives. Before long, the guys rejoined us and, accompanying our conversation with soft picking on his acoustic guitar, Travis answered our questions about his job at the Gibson factory.

"It's much less glamourous than you'd think," he grinned with his usual gentle humility, "although they have been letting me test out a few of the finished guitars before shipping them off to musicians whose names you would definitely know."

The memory of that hum of riffs and beloved voices was interrupted by Pierre's teasing voice calling over the sound of running water, "You're not falling back to sleep, are you, honey?"

"No, no. I'm up," I said. Wrapping the hotel blanket around me, I tiptoed across the cold, thin carpet, pulled open the rubber-backed orange curtain and looked out onto a barren, icy parking lot. My mind drifted back to Diane and Travis.

We left our friends in Bozeman after a neighbourhood walk and breakfast of Wonder Scrambles at their favourite art-filled CatEye Café. The following eight hours hummed by in a fast-paced blur. The freeway was bordered by wide-open shaved corn and soybean fields, last season's stubble poking up through dirty grey snow. I napped off and on throughout the day, while Pierre tuned in to sporadic radio stations, searching for the blues. Montana slid into North Dakota with views of far-distant mountains and mesas. Half way across the long straight stretch of I-94 that bisects North Dakota, we crossed the Missouri River and dropped into an exhausted stupor at Bismarck's Day's Inn.

Behind me, I heard Pierre fill Porter's bowl with kibble and warm water.

"You taking a shower this morning?" he asked. "'Cause if so, you ought to get to it. We've got one last long day of driving ahead, and traffic through Toronto can be atrocious. Not sure whether it's possible, but it would be nice to get home before dark."

Kissing his warm, damp neck on the way by and thanking him for feeding the pup, I hopped into the tiny shower stall and let my mind continue to wander.

On the trip from Bismarck to Minneapolis, we passed through frozen Fargo, where the temperature hit a low of -9°F/-23°C and where we began the southern route around the Great Lakes. Winding through rolling hills and past dozens of small lakes, I was reminded of the many times my college friend had described the beauty of her adopted state of Minnesota. It was, indeed, rustic and post-card picturesque.

Following my carefully mapped directions onto the winding freeways and dark urban streets of Minneapolis, we took only a couple of wrong turns, and finally pulled up in front of Monique and Pat's charming yellow home. Watching two sets of my oldest friends within two days embrace Pierre into their families and seeing him relax in the presence of their kindness and quick intelligence warmed my heart.

Patrick, pulling out all the stops on his chef skills, presented a succulent five course Italian feast at their homey dining table. Knowing that the four of us share an appreciation for bold red wines, we had set aside some of our top California bottles exclusively for that evening. Savouring the last nibbles of brie and blue cheese and our final sips of the third bottle, a *J Winery* Pinotage from the Russian River Valley, Monique pushed back her chair and stood up.

"I have a surprise for you, *if* you're up for going out, that is." Her powerful gaze moved around the table checking our reactions.

Pat lifted a hand in apology. "As much as I'd love to, I have work way too early, but feel free to go without me. Opie and Porter will keep me company." We'd been warned that Opie, their new "recycled" terrier/pug cross (whom they had literally found in a recycling bin) might be a little testy with another male dog in his house. To everyone's delight, they had almost instantly become pals, and we had enjoyed their antics all evening.

Pierre and I both agreed to an adventure, so Monique called for a taxi. Laughing and satiated, we spent the next few hours dancing at Monique's favourite pub. Our timing could not have been better.

Their dear friend's reggae band was booked for a one-night performance, and those four talented guys kept us gleefully on our feet until last call. Ah! It was such a delicious contrast from sitting in the car and a strong reminder of how much I missed dancing.

Porter barely lifted his head upon our return. He was happily exhausted after hours of romping in the yard and playing bitey-face with Opie. It had been our first real exercise in days. Tucking into their spare room at nearly 2:30 AM, Pierre and I gave each other long hugs, rolled apart, and were sound asleep within moments.

Brrr... shivering, I tried to turn the shower tap further toward the red dot and realized it had already hit the max; the hot water tank was empty. Ten minutes later, seeing that Pierre had loaded his backpack into the car, I jammed yesterday's sweats and my toiletry kit into its matching red canvas suitcase. Hoisting Porter's bowls, bag of kibble, and giant dog bed, I once again headed for the car. Pierre was right behind me with my luggage and Porter tugging at the leash. Both of them were geared up for our final ten-hour push. I could see the longing for this passage to be over in the muscles around Pierre's eyes.

Lansing, Michigan, was covered in a light dusting of snow and was surprisingly mild compared to yesterday's frigid and blustery morning in Minneapolis. We loaded the bags behind our seats and followed Porter around the parking lot to the back of the hotel for him to have a quick romp. Even at this hour, I couldn't help but laugh as he pranced back to the car. *Cold toes, cold toes* he seemed to be saying, his tongue lolling and plumes of breath trailing behind. It felt great to laugh.

"So, today's the day," Pierre said, pulling out onto I-69, breakfast sandwiches in hand and steaming cups propped between our seats and knees. "How are you feeling?"

I sipped my scalding tea and squinted out over the frosty, flat landscape. "I'm not awake enough yet to either worry or pray, and I kind of like that. Give me half an hour, ok?"

My driver, my love, smiled with understanding. I smiled back, grateful for his compassion, and turned the heat a little higher. Sinking into the seat and closing my eyes against the bright sunrise, I thought back on yesterday's travels.

It was our longest drive – waking up half hung over and then rolling through five states in one day. The highlight was stopping in Madison, Wisconsin, to finally meet in person our online friend, Lee. Over the prior year, I had spent hours chatting with her in Second Life and listening to her extensive library of rock and blues music as she worked as a DJ in that virtual world. In her real life, Lee was a psychologist, researching and teaching at a university. With my degree in psychology and our mutual interest in healthy relationships, we found rich fodder for long, deep discussions. Also, like us, Lee had met her life partner, Randy, on Second Life, and they were in the planning stages of merging their families.

Meeting at a tiny coffee shop near the university in Madison, we discovered that the captivating connection we had online translated easily into the real world. Our hour together was quickly gone. Through warm hugs, we all expressed a wish for more time together, but her work schedule and the road were calling.

We weathered the only snowstorm of the trip just after sunset while maneuvering through the thick traffic of Chicago's highways. The snow stopped outside Gary, Indiana, just as we left the artificially-lit urban sprawl at the southern tip of Lake Michigan. Exhausted, we sang and told goofy stories to keep ourselves awake the four dark hours before landing at last night's hotel.

After discussing the best- and worst-case scenarios of the upcoming border crossing, I finished the last of my now-cold tea and reached for Pierre's hand. Our passports and document file were tucked beside the seat. Porter's health certificate, my business licenses, plus proof of a U.S. home to return to and sufficient income were all ready for inspection. I was in the driver's seat, since my name was on the vehicle's registration. We inched forward in a line of cars at the Port Huron border crossing, overlooking the arch of the Blue Water Bridge spanning the St. Clair River. Across that narrow strip of freezing water was Pierre's country and a province I'd only seen once: the place I hoped to call home. With the support of friends, family, and my generous group of spiritual partners, I was praying.

A silver SUV pulled away and our signal light turned green. Pierre released my hand, and we each took a deep breath. The fifty-foot drive to the booth felt surreal. An unsmiling charcoal-uniformed officer with a bullet-proof vest tucked his head down and took a long look at us both.

"Good morning," he said, reaching for our passports, "Where ya' headed?"

Chapter 8

March 2009

*J*ust tell them you're going to visit friends for the day.
I thought back on the half-dozen people who had made that suggestion. *They'll never know, and they'll have no idea where to find you.* Childhood memories of Vietnam War draft dodgers stealing across the border rose to the surface when I heard those words. But I wasn't escaping to Canada from the horrors of war. *Besides*, I thought, *I was the worst liar. And what would happen if they caught me?* The answer was clear. No, there would be no lying on this journey.

The border officer's gaze shifted quickly from our passports back to my face when he heard how long I wanted to stay.

"Six months? What are you going to do for six months?"

Pierre and I had rehearsed this. With a small smile, I said, "Travel around Canada. Look for a school to attend." With my heart pounding so hard, I was certain he would see the fabric of my sweater bouncing, I recalled Pierre's suggestions: pretend you're in a courtroom; keep your answers brief and calm; don't go into detail; and, above all, *don't give them any threads to pull.*

"You'll need to go inside and talk to an officer," he replied, handing back our navy-blue passports and vaguely pointing at a row of squat buildings. "Just park over there and go through those doors."

"Yes sir," I gulped. He didn't even glance at Porter who, wanting to meet this stranger, was panting behind my left ear.

Picking a door and moving inside with our envelope of documents clutched against my chest, we were surprised at the absence of a queue. Standing at the fraying taped "Wait Here" line in the middle of the room, we watched as the lone officer shuffled a stack of papers, turned and spoke with someone behind a half-opened door, typed for a minute or two on his computer, then finally looked up and signaled us to his window. Somewhere in his sixties, he gave off the fatigued energy of a retired cop, his deeply furrowed brow above narrowed eyes still watching for deceit and wrong-doing. Broad jawed and stout, his bearing was no-nonsense, about as removed from warm-and-fuzzy as one could get.

"What can I do for you?" he asked in a quick, gravelly voice, without a trace of desire to be of service in either expression or tone.

Just say Yes! I thought. *Please. Let me in.* I set the envelope between us on his narrow beige counter. "I'd like to visit Canada for six months, please," I answered.

He grilled us for the next twenty minutes. Where did we come from? Why did I want to stay so long? Where would I live? How had we met? Where were we planning to travel? Did I have sufficient funds to support this vacation? Was I planning to work? Did I have a home and job to go back to? Why did I need six months to find a school to attend? Did my health insurance cover me in Canada? And on and on.

After every answer, he waited, baiting me with his silence, attempting to lure me into a confession or to trip me up in a lie. I pictured him as a detective interrogating a suspect; this time, that suspect was me. He meticulously examined each page I presented: bank statements from both Pierre's and my banks; business licenses; rental property deeds; Porter's vet clearance; my health insurance card.

The immigration lawyer had neglected to mention health insurance coverage. In truth, I had no idea whether my policy would cover me outside of the states, but Ottawa was only an hour from the New York border. If anything happened, we could always go there, right? I told him I was covered. I could feel the sweat dripping down my back.

"You know," he said grimly, "another officer might turn you back. It sounds like you are planning to come to Canada to *stay* with your boyfriend, not to return when your visitor's permit expires."

"I'm completely willing to go home at the end of six months… if I haven't found a school program that I like," I answered, barely able to breathe.

He stood absolutely still, gazing at me without expression. The silence grew.

We didn't move.

"I'll give you a month," he finally said, his index fingers clacking across his keyboard. "It shouldn't take you longer than that to find a school. If it does, come back to the border and apply for an extension."

Blinking back tears, a lump formed in my throat as I swallowed a yelped protest.

"If you *do* file for an extension, since you're both self-employed, bring back more proof of income and a copy of your health insurance policy."

He walked abruptly away from the counter with a sniff and a minute later brought back an official-looking document. Stapling it into my passport, and folding it just so, he looked at us over the tops of his glasses. He cleared his throat. "The expiry date on this visitor permit is binding. If you do not return to the United States, extend the deadline, or get a study permit, you will be violating Canadian law and could be permanently deported. Do you understand?"

Nodding, I carefully packed my documents back into their envelope. "Thank you, sir," I said over my shoulder as we moved away from his window. He neither looked up nor replied. Back outside, tears of both relief and disappointment rolled down my cheeks. *One month? And then we'd have to go through this again?*

I barely noticed when Pierre unlocked the car and tossed the envelope onto the seat. He turned and lifted me off the ground in a tight hug, then kissed my tears away, whispering, "Sweetie, you're *in!*" Moments later, with a tentative smile on my face, we climbed back into the Passat with Porter for our final leg home.

Three weeks later ~

Porter and I both scooted near the heater, having just returned from a frosty romp at Saint Paul U's unofficial dog park. Settling in at our new dining room table, I checked our paperwork for the umpteenth time. *Please let this work,* I prayed, thumbing through the sections of the blue presentation folder. It was Saturday morning, the day we were driving down to the New York border crossing.

In an odd but ideal flash of synchronicity, Pierre began a new contract just after my arrival; he was now working with the Immigration and Refugee Board of Canada. A few days after starting, he emailed me a giant public document from his new department's website, which outlined in minute detail the regulations and requirements for new immigrants. Over the next few years I would learn just how fluid those rules were, as the department implemented a never-ending stream of updates, amendments, and modifications.

Following those initial guidelines, we collected and organized a file presenting our best case. Arranged in our thick blue folder was evidence that I wasn't impoverished, looking to drain Canada's extensive welfare or health care systems, or the type of person who would steal a citizen's job. Tax and bank records showed that even without my savings and investments, Pierre could support us. In addition, to my relief, a bulky envelope from Blue Cross arrived on Thursday verifying that my health insurance covered me no matter where I travelled.

"Look here," the binder was meant to say, "Patrice isn't a threat. She is a responsible U.S. citizen who is willing to return home at the end of her allotted stay. She is visiting her boyfriend and wants to stay here until college begins in September." We knew this was true. The proof was all there. Still, they *could* say no.

Our drive to the border was electric and quiet. On either side of Highway 416 black-branched trees stood out stark against the white sky. Everything was buckled down, still and sharp, the soft greens poised to arrive, but still under the surface awaiting the spring.

Upon arrival, we visited the washrooms, which inexplicably stood a short walk away from the main building. As I sat praying in the privacy of a stall, the outside door screeched open and someone else entered the room. Sighing, I got up to wash my hands and was startled to see a uniformed border officer joining me at the sinks. Our eyes met in the mirror as she slicked back her dark hair with her damp hands, tucking unruly curls back into a plain black hair tie. As we dried our hands together on the rough paper towels, she asked why I was there. When I said that I wanted to extend my visitor's permit, her reply floored me.

"Oh. No, sorry. You can't do that here. You have to apply by mail to Mississauga." Her voice, though matter-of-fact, held a surprising trace of genuine regret.

"But we were told in Sarnia that we had to return to the border to get an extension."

We left the washroom and joined Pierre, who was waiting on the walkway.

"No," she said again, as we followed her through the biting wind into the main brick building. "You have to mail in your request at least one month prior to your current permit's expiry date."

"But my current permit is only *for* one month!" I caught the near-whine in my voice and composed myself. "The border officer gave me one month to gather more information and said to come here to request a five-month extension." I refused to believe that the Sarnia officer would have lied to us. Perhaps it wasn't the usual practice to give these extensions in person, but I knew it could be done.

Shaking her head as she settled beside her computer, she reiterated, "We don't give visitor extensions here."

Slowly I placed our folder on the familiar beige counter and looking at her, reached for Pierre's hand.

"Well, let me take a look at what you have," she said, her scrubbed face above the official charcoal tie showing more kindness and curiosity than I had anticipated.

I explained that we had driven across the continent and narrated our experience at Sarnia and then, with slightly trembling hands, walked her page-by-page through our packet. A few sheets shy of the end she rested her hand on the folio and smiled.

"This is not something we normally do," she said, "but all of this is great. I think we can make this happen for you today."

I nearly jumped across the counter to kiss her, but instead, Pierre and I slid into an embrace, both of us misty-eyed. A short while later, she removed the original permit from my passport and stapled in a new one, again folding it in the official pattern and handed it back with a warm smile.

"Enjoy your stay. I am required to remind you that the expiry date on your permit is binding. Once you have been accepted to a college program, bring the original acceptance letter here to the border and we will issue you a study permit. If you do not find a program or decide not to study, you can apply to extend this visitor's permit again by mailing it in prior to its expiry." She lowered her voice, "I wish you luck. Please don't try to bypass any steps or attempt to work under the table. There are many things that could prevent your immigration process, and I would hate to see that happen." She shook our hands, and we were on our way.

Chattering through giant grins as I practically skipped back to the car, Pierre suggested that a celebration might be in order. Taking the scenic drive along the winding River Road south of Ottawa, we stopped at a place that would become one of our favourites, The Swan on the Rideau. There, looking out on the marina through the bare branches of an immense maple tree, we drank a toast to kind border officials and to the next chapter of our lives together.

Patrice Lefebvre

Chapter 9

May 2009   Two months later

This morning, like every weekday morning, I watched Pierre transform from my cuddly sweetheart into the businessman that most others know. He donned his slacks and button-down-collar shirt, clipped on his security pass, tucked his phone into his breast pocket, then stepped into his dress shoes and headed out the door. After our goodbye kisses, nine hours loomed with only two dog walks on my schedule; otherwise the calendar was as vacant as fresh fields of snow awaiting the crunch of boots.

Returning from our first walk, I unclipped Porter's lead, wandered into the small, galley-style kitchen, and filled the teapot.

"What sounds good for breakfast, mister?" I asked, knowing exactly what his would be. "How do you like having the same delicious kibble every meal? You like that? Yeah!"

Porter's tail thumped a rhythm on the cupboard below the sink. I filled his bowl and added warm water. Setting it next to his water dish, I put him through his paces: sit, down, shake, sit pretty. He panted, baring a happy smile with each accomplishment.

"OKAY!" I said, snickering as he dove from sitting on his back legs, nose first into his meal. "Ah, what a treat it would be to live such a simple life." My words were barely audible over his sloppy scarfing.

Choosing a variety of veggies to make a brunch frittata, I surveyed the contents of the fridge and thought about Pierre's response to my fledgling cooking skills. I wasn't sure whether he actually *liked* what I made, or whether he was so thrilled at not having to be the chef, that he raved about every dish. Regardless, his loving enthusiasm was encouraging, and I was enjoying the creativity of finding and making new recipes. It felt great to make Pierre happy and to contribute to our household with sweat equity. In addition to my family's old standby meals, I was building a file of keepers, and, living with a French Canadian, had learned to make a mean lump-free gravy.

Finished with brunch, I tucked under a quilt on our gently-used sofa. Looking around the silent living room, I wondered again how long it would be before I found friends in this town. Besides my evening and weekend tête-à-têtes with Pierre, most of my interactions took place at the dog park. Those chats were brief, at least on my end, and dog-centered. Yesterday afternoon I had once again answered the standard opening question about Porter's age with, "He's almost 11; how about yours?" only to get stuck nodding to fifteen minutes of not-a-break-in-sight stories about Muffy or Peanut or Zeus. For weeks now, none of my attempts to expand into other subjects had been met with more than a passing interest. Eventually, conversation would fall away or – like yesterday – I would interrupt with an excuse to continue walking or just head home. I didn't expect it to be easy to find balanced and varied friendships but was determined to do so; I just wasn't sure where or how it would happen. Luckily, I enjoyed alone time, so although I rarely felt lonely, I *was* beginning to get bored.

I spent part of each day checking in with friends on email and Facebook. *It was odd, though*, I thought, scrolling through status updates, *barely talking with anyone but Pierre or Porter for days on end*. I missed the sounds of my friends' voices and laughter and the warm familiarity of sharing intimate thoughts and meals with well-known beloved people. Since they all had jobs, talking on Skype mid-day wasn't really an option. I was especially grateful for the ongoing CSL Connection Circle. So far there hadn't been even one sign of a New Thought church here. No Unity. No Church of Religious Science or Centre for Spiritual Living. Pierre had been right. There were many traditional churches but finding people whose spiritual practice came from an alternative perspective might be more problematic than I'd hoped.

Second Life, I found, was bland without Pierre, so after a couple of visits, I let that go. A few weekends before, we had gone in together, sitting at either end of the soft cream sofa with our laptops. Within half an hour of watching our avatars dance and typing inane instant messages, we looked across the four-foot span, cracked up, and shut the computers down to resume real life.

That said, I felt extremely grateful for the Internet. In addition to meeting Pierre there, I was gaining a rough understanding of the immigration process and had found possibilities for college programs starting in the fall. While surfing the 'net for local happenings, I found Canada's Craigslist, a free ad site called Kijiji. The new hide-a-bed couch and a comfy leather arm chair were our best discoveries to date; at least as far as used furniture went. I was learning that, like me, Pierre had expensive taste. The distinction was, he had long been able to afford more expensive things and was accustomed to finding values – not at thrift stores, but by thoroughly researching Consumer Reports and shopping online. Last night we discussed it over a bottle of peppery Petit Syrah.

"I think I've done more shopping in the past month than in the past five years combined. Getting a little burnt out on it; how about you?"

"No kidding!" I said, "Maybe we can have a *buy nothing* weekend this coming one?"

"To two full days of *no new stuff!*" He laughed and raised his glass, "Although... we do need to find a rug for this living room... and maybe the bedroom... but they can wait until next week." We toasted, and each took a sip.

"I'm excited for Thursday's delivery, though. I think the new coffee and end tables will be beautiful in here and are going to go great with the dining set. And I love it that we agreed so easily on the craftsman style."

"You've got good taste," he said, grinning. "It is starting to feel like a home in here, isn't it? And those apple cinnamon candles were an excellent idea to clear out the fumes. I never would have thought of that."

"I'm just glad it worked," I said, smiling. It was touching that he cared so much about whether I would like the apartment he had found. Honestly, it had felt homey, even though nearly empty, from the moment I'd stepped through the door.

My mind drifted to that moment and our last day of driving across Ontario. The landscape had been peaceful: flat, snow-covered fields and a few low rolling hills dotted with evergreens and bare deciduous trees.

"Enjoy this while you can," Pierre warned me, "Toronto's traffic along the 401 is a race car driver's torment. The stretch between Mississauga and Pickering is nearly always gridlocked. What would be a forty-five-minute drive in Ottawa will probably take *a lot* longer."

Sure enough, we crawled for almost three hours, at one point in the middle of eight lanes of cars traveling each direction. I was reminded of Seattle's long, crowded rush hours, and seeing Pierre's tight jaw and constant manoeuvring, was pleased he would not be subjected to them. We arrived at Hazel Street at almost midnight, exhausted, but thrilled to be home.

Blinking back to the present, my eyes followed two chattering women as they and their dogs passed by our front windows. A rare twist of envy tightened like a band across my chest. I shook my head and turned back to the computer screen. I would not indulge in a pity party; instead, I would be happy for those women and their easy friendship. I knew how to attract fantastic things and whining about the things *not yet* in my life definitely wasn't part of that practice. My new friends were out there. I just needed to know that, be open to unexpected opportunities, and imagine the joy and gratitude that having those friendships would bring.

Looking down at my fingers resting on the keyboard, it suddenly occurred to me that the Internet might be a portal to local connections. Re-opening Kijiji, I perused the personals section. Hmm... Women Seeking Women. Scrolling slowly through the lesbians' listings – some carefully veiled, others fearlessly out – I came upon a pink-bordered commercial ad for an Ottawa-based website called Girlfriend Social. Clicking its link and looking over the professionally-designed home page, I murmured, *Brilliant! I wish I had thought of this!* As I read through the guidelines and created a profile, I found myself giggling at the idea. *Who would have guessed that there was a Match.com for straight women? Right here in my new town and free to boot!* There were fewer than a thousand members; it seemed the site had just gone live a couple of months before. The owner did a meticulous job with the search options and, by entering an age range and a few of my own interests, a short list of matches appeared. Reading carefully through the profiles, I found two women who sounded like my kind of people: powerful, funny, and insightful.

Vickie, who had also moved here recently, was a novice roller blader and avid reader, who was interested in metaphysical and personal development. *Perhaps it wouldn't be so difficult to find spiritual friends, after all!* I thought. Catherine loved to dance at local clubs and sounded as though she was up for learning almost anything new. Both of them were moms of independent adult children and, surprisingly, both had rescued Shih Tzus. Porter loved small pups; maybe we would both meet new friends. Sending both women quick emails through the website, I glanced down at the clock in the corner of my screen. As had happened many times on Second Life, three hours had flown by.

Setting the computer aside, I watched as Porter hauled himself up off his bed and began to pace back and forth between me and the front door, claws clicking on the oak floors. His meaning was clear, though his movements were slower here. In Washington, we had lived on carpeted floors. Whether due to his age, the slippery hardwood, or unexpected patches of ice, he seemed to be a little more cautious these days. It was finally warm enough that we could forego his plaid flannel jacket and the purple rubber booties that protected his feet from ice and salt. Sliding into my coat and boots and clipping on his leash, we headed out on our afternoon walk.

Two blocks up the street, at the entrance to Saint Paul University's grounds, Porter sniffed the base of a new addition, a ten-foot-tall, temporary black sign with neon coloured stick-on letters. "MAIN EVENT!" it declared. "Don't Miss Old Ottawa East's Community Event of the Year! Saturday, June 13, 2009. Main Farmers Market, Wagon Rides, Bouncy Castle, Craft

Fair, Used Book Sale. Visit OttawaEast.ca for more information." Snapping a photo of the sign, I resumed our trudge through the soggy, sour-smelling field to the back of the Oblates' residence where a dozen dogs played. His tail going non-stop, Porter greeted each pup in turn and splashed through the molding tan grass and puddles of melted snow. An hour later, toweled dry, he crawled back onto his puffy bed in our living room, sighed, and a few moments later was snoring.

That evening after cleaning up the dinner dishes, I tucked under the blanket next to Pierre on the sofa and opened my laptop to share the afternoon's saved tabs.

"Check this out, sweetie," I said. "I found some amazing things online today."

Scrolling through our neighbourhood's community site, I showed him a listing for the upcoming street fair and book sale.

"A used book sale; nice," he said. "Ottawa has lots of them, and you can get some excellent deals, a quarter or even a dime for some books."

"They have a call out for volunteers to help organize and prepare for it, and I emailed the coordinator. She wrote back right away and sounded delightful! I'll be meeting her at the Old Town Hall next Wednesday."

"Right on, honey. That sounds like it will be right up your alley."

I closed the Old Ottawa East community site and the Algonquin College website appeared. Walking with him through my marked tabs, we explored the International Student pages and three certificate programs: Scriptwriting, Journalism, and Professional Writing. Upon initial read-through, I had nearly eliminated scriptwriting, since I didn't watch television, although we *did* rent lots of Blockbuster movies. In discussing the program, we learned that we both enjoyed seeing an occasional play, but neither of us had ever been involved in theatre. In the end, we decided it wasn't enough of a fit, and crossed scriptwriting off the list.

Journalism seemed as though it might be a dying industry, but I felt it was worth further exploration. As Pierre and I studied and talked about the two programs, the variety of the Professional Writing courses looked more and more attractive. From fiction to government and business writing classes, certainly I could find a style that would be right for me. Jotting down the phone numbers for the coordinators of the two programs, I planned to call them both in the morning.

Closing Algonquin's website, the final tab, Girlfriend Social, popped into view. I clapped when I saw a red flag on the site's inbox icon. We had talked

about the concept over dinner, so before showing him
Vickie and Catherine's profile pages, I opened the
email. It read:

> Hello Patrice,
>
> Thank you for writing. I too just moved to Ottawa
> (from Kamloops—not that far from Seattle!)
> though I lived here and in Montreal for many years
> before moving to BC. It's great to be back, but the
> only person I know here is my boyfriend. That's
> why I joined GFS. Would you be interested in
> meeting somewhere for a walk or for tea (or coffee,
> if you'd prefer)?
>
> Looking forward to your reply,
>
> Vickie

My pulse raced as I re-read it out loud to Pierre.
He wrapped me in a hug before disappearing into the
kitchen. Returning a moment later, he set two glasses
and a bottle of wine on the floor in front of us.

"I know we're drinking too much," he said, filling
our glasses with a fragrant, nearly-black Syrah, "but it
feels as if there is cause for celebration every day!" He
handed a glass to me and raised his in a toast. "Sounds
as though your quiet afternoons are about to be over,
and I will be sharing you with a bunch of new people,"

he said with a grin. "To great friendships and exciting adventures. *Sante!*"

Chapter 10

August 2009   Three months later

From: Patrice Elston
Date: Saturday, Aug 1, 2009 11:14 PM
To: CSL Connection Circle
Subject: Patrice's Gratitudes and Check-in

Dear *Seattle Center for Spiritual Living* Connection Circle,

I'm writing on the evening of my mom's birthday from my sister's familiar, cool basement on the shore of Moses Lake. What a whirlwind this past week has been! Pierre is already sound asleep, and I'm not long behind him. Such a wonderful man to bring me back for a vacation so soon after my move to Ottawa. I am constantly learning more about generosity from my dear Pierre.

We packed a boatload of visits into our stay in Seattle, including one-on-one lunches, dinners, and teas with a bunch of friends and family. Our dear friend, Jan, generously hosted a grand backyard pizza party that was attended by a dozen friends. Nearly everyone was meeting Pierre for the first time. It felt as though we all connected easily, as if we'd been apart only a few days and, as expected, Pierre was his usual charming self. I've been teasing him about the exponential growth of his fan club! I am so grateful that he has such an open heart.

His easy-going nature shone again when we visited the peninsula. I'd been eager to share my former commute – the breathtaking ferry ride and drive out to Poulsbo – and show Pierre the small farm where I had lived the ten years prior to my divorce. There, I was able to love up my kitties, who seemed to remember me, and who I hope have forgiven me for leaving them behind. My "wasbund" (who graciously accepted my request for a visit) gave Pierre a tour of the farm, and we continued chatting over lunch at Los Cabos, one of our favourite cafes in town. Watching their first interactions, I once again gave thanks that they are the men that they are. Clearly, they have both done the work that it takes to be gentle and respectful in what could have been an extremely tense situation. Thank you for your help in keeping me grounded through this, dear prayer partners. As you know, I went in and out of worry around this meeting and knowing that you were holding us in prayer helped me flow with it.

The past four days here with the family have been as eventful as the previous ones were in Seattle. The first two, Pierre was put to work helping Dad build a dividing wall in Gramps' garage – in the 100-degree heat – and Mom and I packed Gramps' belongings into boxes, as my folks are turning his home into a rental. Being handed a hammer was a somewhat startling introduction to our family's traditional work parties, and I was grateful that Pierre stepped in without complaint – at least not publicly. Discussing it in bed that first night, I was amazed to hear that it had shocked him to be expected to work on his vacation. I hadn't given the work party a second thought. Helping out with projects was just what family did. It's fascinating to discover the differences in our lives, and always interesting to see how each of us assimilate our history, and then assume that our patterns are the norm.

As I've mentioned before, Pierre is unaccustomed to a closely bonded family, so I've been watching him take lots of room to observe (as if he could get a word in edgewise!) as he finds his place in the clan. My family grew used to my former husband's exuberant partying nature, and Pierre's calm demeanor seems to be an adjustment for everyone. I've not seen any trace of animosity, more a quiet curiosity, for which I am grateful.

Yesterday we visited Gramps at his care facility. After looking up from his nap to see who was coming through the front doors, he recognized me right away. So heartwarming! Mom says that both his hearing and dementia have worsened, so I was praying for this outcome. I showed him photos of our life in Ottawa on my laptop, which I think he enjoyed, although he seemed to find it somewhat confusing. "It's hell to get old," he said with his signature grin. I hope that is not true for all of us. I know some of you have family members with dementia and can relate to my feelings of joy at every step forward and grief at each further loss. I feel truly blessed that we were able to spend time with my dear Gramps, and that, at this point, he is still mostly present.

Other highlights here included celebrating two birthdays, (my mom's and my eldest grand-nephew, Brodee's); Pierre waterskiing behind my nephew's boat – his first time in over twenty years; and today's visit to a chimpanzee rehabilitation facility. If any of you get the chance to cross the mountains to visit Central Washington University's *Chimposium*, I highly recommend it. The group of us using sign language to communicate "hug/love," "friend," and "sorry" to calm an agitated 200-pound primate, as he hurled himself at the Plexiglas wall between us was an incredible experience. The rescued chimps, Loulis, Tatu, and especially Dar, with his sweet freckled face, will remain in my memories for many years. From the lecture we attended, it seems that the chimpanzees, while learning sign language from the students, are teaching the students about community and respect in ways that are deeply affecting the young people's lives.

Speaking of education, everyone has been full of congratulations upon hearing of my acceptance into the Professional Writing program. The application process was stressful, although looking back, I imagine the college welcomes as many international students as possible. With tuition three times the cost of a Canadian's, we foreigners must be a bit of a cash cow for the institutions.

Writing and re-writing my 500-word application, filling out college forms, and the back-to-school procedure – paying tuition, figuring out health insurance, parking permitting, finding a dog-sitter, not to mention *yet another* trip to the border – added up to a mind-boggling folder of information. *One step at a time*, I can hear you all saying. I'm certain that your reminders helped me to breathe and visualize positive outcomes. I will admit, though, that until the border officer replaced my visitor permit with a two-year student permit, I chased away fears nearly every day. It was a comfort knowing you were praying for me, as I was for each of you.

Thank you for sending your updates and gratitudes. I love hearing your adventures, your blessings and challenges, and the ways in which I can support you in visualization and prayer.

My requests this week... May our upcoming week's travels in California be safe and fulfilling, and may my friends and family remain healthy and know, without doubt, how very loved they are.

Sending serenity and blessings,

Patrice

Chapter 11

August 2009

"I feel as though I took that left turn at Albuquerque."

"Whaat?" I say, gazing out over the road winding through gorgeous Napa Valley hills and past rich green vineyards. This is definitely not New Mexico.

Pierre's deep laugh fills the car. "Bugs Bunny, hon'," he says, and I chuckle along with him. It's one of his funny habits: a tendency to be goofy, to regularly break out in song lyrics or movie lines. I get most of his references; however, since Looney Tunes re-runs played afternoons on CBC well into his young adulthood, he and many Canadians can quote practically every Bugs episode verbatim. The last time I watched those cartoons I was probably 10 years old, curled up on Saturday mornings in my jammies with a bowl of cereal. My being deprived of such easy familiarity with these classics seems somewhat disturbing to him.

"What I mean is, everything in my life has changed. You cannot know what a relief it is to no longer feel that every problem is my fault, that I can never find the right solutions. I wondered for years whether I was even lovable. Now, I am amazed at feeling this loved – cherished, even."

I reach across and take his hand – often resting on the gear shift, manual or not – and lift it to my lips. Looking back up at him I see the glistening in his eyes.

"I never dreamed I would be with someone who wanted to hear about my work, my thoughts, even my car obsession." Again, we grin at each other. "And the things you introduce me to! A year ago, no one could have guessed where we spent the day today. Certainly not I."

Looking out on a long tunnel of eucalyptus trees, I think back to the day he proposed this vacation. I had only been in Ottawa for a couple of months, and every day I could hear the West Coast calling. We scrolled through photos and reminisced over fantastic memories of our previous trip to central California, dreaming of returning to the wineries and beaches. I'll never forget the feeling when he looked up from the computer and asked if I'd like to go back right away.

"Are you *serious*?" My reluctance to believe was palpable.

"Absolutely! We have a little extra in the coffers since I'm not racing this season, and we can book it at a time when I'll lose the least number of days on my contract. How would you feel about a week in Washington and a week in California?"

I actually leapt into his arms. As we began talking about all the people I wanted to see in Washington, we realized that this was probably not going to be a relaxing vacation. Discussing it further, we decided that spending the second week north of San Francisco at my timeshare in Sonoma would give us the chance to unwind after a whirlwind first week.

"... in addition to wine tasting, we can spend some time in the city, I can take you to the Wharf, show you my old flat in the Haight Ashbury district, go out to Ocean Beach, and... oh my God! We can go up to Harbin!" Okay, so maybe both weeks would be busy, but at least we could be on our own schedule in California.

Today, Pierre found out why Harbin Hot Springs is one of my "heavens on Earth." We spent the last seven hours in the California sun surrounded by dusty oak-covered hills and beautiful naked people of all shapes and sizes.

As it was Pierre's first time in a clothing-optional place, I told him about my experiences with nude beaches and hot springs, my astonishment at the lack of sexual tension and judgement. There had been none of that competitive anxiety which seemed rampant at bikini beaches. My gut feeling says that being naked in nature with strangers takes a certain level of self-love and bravery. Harbin is such a healing place; its residents and visitors mingle in near-silent gentleness and acceptance. I relish that rarely-found environment of mutual vulnerability. Walking slowly up the stairs to the main pool, Pierre squeezed my hand.

"This feels so *right*," he said. "What could be more natural than this?"

Upon arrival, we'd been shyly greeted by a black-tailed doe and her twin fawns in the parking area. Wandering between natural wood and soft blue painted buildings, I pointed out each trail leading to lodging, cafes, and the yoga temple. I held Pierre's hand as the trail opened into the main pool area. His fingers softened as we stood and soaked in the view. The serenity was palpable.

After tucking our clothes into alcoves, the wood worn smooth by years of use, we met back outside the cozy dressing rooms and began our visit in earnest. We washed off the dust under outdoor showers, soaked in various-temperature natural pools, and ate flavourful salads with ingredients grown in the lush gardens. Soft-voiced conversations drifted around us. The pace slowed more and more as we tuned into Harbin's rhythm.

Mid-afternoon I treated us to our scheduled *piece de resistance*: Watsus. For an hour we were each held, stretched, pushed, and pulled through the warm water of a large secluded pool, cradled and massaged by the water and the strong hands of our Water Shiatsu practitioners. Partway through I opened my eyes to gaze across the clear expanse to watch Pierre's treatment. The blissful smile on his face as he was drawn through the water in a slow-motion dance confirmed what I had hoped: he was relishing this just as I was. As if he could feel me watching, his eyelids fluttered open, eyes meeting mine. His smile spread wide, then his lips pursed into a silent kiss before he sank back into peaceful meditation. Although I had visited this community dozens of times, sharing it with Pierre was by far the most idyllic.

"This place is my ideal church," I whispered later, as we rested on beach towels on a huge redwood deck.

"It's a hundred and eighty degrees from the Catholic services I walked away from more than thirty years ago, that's for sure," he quietly replied, "and a church I could imagine attending regularly."

Opening my water bottle, filled at the icy spring-fed fountain, I took a long drink then offered it to Pierre. He smiled, shaking his head and nodding at the sharp curves ahead. This section of the road called for both hands on the wheel.

Over the past few weeks I have been opening up more about my life philosophy and spiritual practice. Every evening I share my daily gratitudes and – although he finds it a little weird – read aloud to him before we fall asleep. He is not much of a reader (except online,) and being such a big-picture guy, he struggles to stay patient with details. The book I chose is *Building Your Field of Dreams*, by one of my favourite teachers, Mary Morrissey. It is full of Christian references, many of which make him roll his eyes and argue, as he has for years, about religious rhetoric. Some nights I participate in his debates, pushing through my reluctance and dialing up my patience to help him understand this teaching with a broader vision, and sometimes I lose it.

"Can't you just replace the words 'God' or 'Jesus' in your mind with 'love' or 'life' or even 'the Universe'?" I ask again. "It's all the same; it includes us; it doesn't care what you call it."

The triggers are strong for both of us, but as we progress through the book, I've noticed fewer arguments and more interest. He knows that when he sets a goal and commits to reaching it, he usually gets it and has trained himself not to let doubts pull him off course. As he begins to set the "God language" aside, he says he is starting to see that others practice his same activities; we just use different language.

"It never occurred to me that being positive and keeping my attention on reaching a goal might be called a manifestation prayer," he said.

"You just didn't know how spiritual you've been all this time," I replied.

"Aw, sweetheart.... Have I told you lately how much I love being with you?" The reading, at least for that night, is over.

To avoid car sickness, I keep my eyes on the road for the most winding portion of the drive back to Sonoma. I know how much Pierre loves driving these roads and feel the car begin to speed up. Glancing in the side-view mirror, I see glimpses of a motorcyclist crouched low, leaning through the curves, slowly gaining on us. Our rented Shaker-blue Mustang could give him some stiff competition, and I see Pierre's shoulders raise a bit, his pulse undoubtedly kicking up. There are only a few miles left before we are back on the straight highway. As he stretches his fingers open on the wheel, he grins into the mirror. I can almost hear him thinking, *Yeah, let's do this* as his foot eases down on the accelerator.

"You okay?" he asks, as we begin to be pulled side to side in the deep seats.

"All good," I say, and reach for the handle above the window. *I trust him. He's a great driver. My stomach is strong.* I chant silently, slowing my breath, keeping my eyes locked on the curve ahead, and let my mind drift.

In the five months I've lived with Pierre, I have begun to realize just how complex he is. Although the traditionally masculine auto racing is deep in his blood, I often forget it when engaged in one of our long, insightful conversations. And yet, he describes himself as a "relatively typical guy." Men, he told me, do not share their deepest thoughts with each other, gab about their women, or set up coffee or dinner dates. They *do* stuff together. Race cars. Play hockey. Look at cars. Make bets over card games. Tinker with engines, suspensions, brakes, and tires. Drink beer.

Last year, after eleven years of playing hockey, sciatica benched him after a fall. He said he misses the exercise, but more so the banter and laughs, both on the ice and the play-by-play deliberations over post-game breakfasts. Occasionally an invitation to a Texas Hold 'Em night arrives, but like me, he has no poker face and his practical side doesn't allow him to throw away money on gambling. He politely declines and tells me in a bittersweet tone that at some point they will probably stop asking. Most of his racing buddies live in and around Toronto, so he has begun researching the local racing scene for opportunities to build more community in Ottawa.

We knew this before I moved, but it's becoming clearer: I am far more social than he is, but I also require more alone time. He hasn't yet witnessed it, but I tend to get "peopled-out" at parties or other major social events. On the other hand, I interact with dozens of friends online. My need to share thoughts and celebrate victories, to hold my friends above water when they struggle to regain footing, hear their insights, and help them express their best selves is almost completely foreign to him. I feel blessed that he steps out of his normally private shell and shares himself with me, as his wisdom and playful soul fills my heart.

We've talked about the difference between my extended family, both blood and not, and his deep-seated independence. When he explained that he was the one to inherit the holiday gatherings when his mother passed, I was thrilled to hear it, until realizing that it probably meant that I wouldn't meet his siblings until Canadian Thanksgiving in October. It's hard to understand their autonomy. I would like to see him reconnect with his sister and spend more time with his brothers and old friends. The truth is, he's made it clear that although he likes them, he has little in common with them. His momentum moves him forward, and reminiscing about old times holds very little appeal.

He and his former wife led a quiet existence. They had few friends and had fallen into a lackluster routine: work, dinner, and sleep on weekdays, chores and mostly separate activities on weekends. The outcome is that he doesn't have much of a social life. Perhaps the biggest disappointment is that his old house has not yet sold, and with all of our recent changes, he's choosing to save money by taking a break from the tracks this year. After eight racing seasons, he misses his friends and track time and speaks in great anticipation of getting back to it next spring and introducing me to the couples who attend together.

I've spent a little time with Vickie and Catherine from the Girlfriend Social site, and the one big neighbourhood event I participated in, the Main Event book sale, brought a small handful of new women into my life. Sadly, it looks as though those friendships may have been temporary. We spent four weeks organizing books alphabetically and by genre, chatting about all kinds of things and finding donated treasures. I was gifted a small box to take home, which I filled with Canadian-author children's books for my grandnephews and a few "to-reads" for me. Pierre and I attended the lively post-event volunteer dinner on the Royal Oak's patio overlooking the canal. The following day, we spent a couple of hours boxing up the leftover books and storing them for their final recycling. Since then, the replies to my touching-base emails have been non-existent or cursory. And so, I move on.

The Kawasaki that reached our tail finally blasts past just as the road levels out. The rider tips his head on the way by and drops his left hand in a three-fingered wave. A few miles later, Pierre flashes the lights when the rider turns right into Santa Rosa, and we head left toward our temporary digs.

"What do you feel like doing tonight, darlin'?" Pierre asks as we settle onto the hum of the final, flat stretch.

"How about just dinner and a video?"

"Sounds great!" he says and points the car toward an ancient taco stand with a stellar reputation. A half hour later we arrive at the timeshare welcome building and, leaving our burritos cooling in a bag on the front seat, we sort through a tall bookshelf of movies for rent. We have discovered that neither of us are fans of the gratuitous violence which makes up much of popular filmmaking, so we pass on the action and super-hero films and discuss the merits of the ones that catch our attention.

Thus far at home Pierre has relented to my twenty-plus-year choice of being television-free. The never-ending reporting of violence in the US news, repetition of crass, disrespectful communication patterns in what passes for comedy, and *Buy-Buy-Buy* of advertising set my teeth on edge. Pierre said he finds being television-free quiet and strange, but not entirely unpleasant, and he's willing to go with this until the hockey and Formula One seasons begin. Then we'll see. Perhaps we will watch a few races or games at a pub; perhaps we will subscribe to cable for a year.

Most, but not all of our compromises have been this simple. After living lives of fierce self-reliance and leadership, I think we both find it difficult to share that role at times, and we have had a few head-butts. One of my favourite spiritual teachers calls it TTSM: Two Tigers, Same Mountain. Lucky for both of us, we are not stone-wallers, manipulators, or shouters. Our mutual goal is to meet somewhere in the middle, to feed our relationship rather than harm it for the sake of winning a trivial argument.

Talking isn't the only thing that's easy between us. I could never have hoped for such a fun and compatible lover, especially not at age fifty! We've decided it's like we're in our twenties again. Only now, with so many years of experiences logged, there is a depth of self-knowledge and compassion to which most twenty-year-olds seem completely oblivious. "Maybe," Pierre said last night, "it is *because* of our age that our relationship is so good." I agreed wholeheartedly.

"It's going to be strange watching a movie without Porter at our feet," Pierre said, handing back a copy of the latest *Beethoven* movie, shaking his head *no* at my suggestion of a comedy of errors played out by a sloppy Saint Bernard. We talked earlier about the peculiarity of being away from home and walking through the door of the timeshare with no pets to greet us. The kennel where we boarded Porter felt as homey as one could get; he would move between play yards, individual pens, and the main house, and I had to trust that he was doing well. He got along with almost everyone, so was probably having a great time.

I watched him carefully when he met my new friend Catherine's puppy, Zoe, who weighed maybe three pounds – not much more than a squirrel – and he was so gentle with her! Even when she was hanging off his ears with her sharp puppy teeth, he took it in stride.

Pierre is excellent with Porter, even though he'd clearly prefer to not have the responsibility of walking and feeding. He sighs when I show him pictures of dogs and cats from the pet adoption sites, but he clearly understands how important animals are to me. I have a feeling he will set a limit, but don't think he'd ever insist that we live pet-free. Porter is in one of his last chapters; perhaps soon we can adopt a pair of kittens to keep him young in his final years.

Marley and Me, the film I'd most like to see, is not yet out in DVD, so we finally settle on Pixar's latest offering, *Wall-E*, and head back out to the car.

Winding slowly past a dozen identical car-bordered buildings, we park outside our unit under a massive live oak. We gather our bags of damp towels, extra clothes, and dinner and trudge up the stairs to our third-floor condo. Pierre pours a couple of glasses of Kendall-Jackson cabernet. I unwrap our fragrant meal, and we relax onto the couch to watch the quixotic animated film about Earth's last robot. Five more days of winery tours and a trip out to the coast await us. I find myself reaching for Pierre's hand again and closing my eyes in a silent prayer of gratitude for this... and for us.

Chapter 12

June 2010   Ten months later

*N*o more wallowing, I thought, adding another tissue to the pile. *Besides, they will all die, too, if I don't get over there; I've got to do this.* I blew my nose again and slowly pulled the covers aside. Standing next to the couch, my gaze dropped to the rumpled nest where I'd holed up the past few days: Gran's embroidered quilt and our soft blue blanket, my pillow that I had dragged out of the bedroom mid-morning, a chipped teapot of cold tea beside my oldest ceramic mug, and a nearly empty box of Kleenex. The Levolor blinds were clamped tight, holding out the summer's blazing heat. I left them closed.

Finding my dirty faded blue jeans on the bedroom floor where I'd stepped out of them at 4:30 Monday morning, I slid them back on, along with the top t-shirt in the drawer. I splashed my face with cold water three, four, five times, and ran my toothbrush around my mouth just enough to mask the morning taste with mint. My hair secured back into a ponytail, I tucked into flip-flops, grabbed my rubber-dipped gloves and sunglasses, stuffed a pocket full of tissues, and pushed myself out the door. Thank goodness there were no other tenants in the lobby.

It took a block for the tears to begin again. Automatically stopping before crossing the street, I looked down to my left to be sure Porter was in a sit. Of course. My breath caught. He wasn't there. My knees let go, melting me to the curb where, instead, I sat cradling my forehead against crossed arms, and let the hot tears flow.

"Miss? Miss. Are you okay?" came a voice behind me.

I dug the wad of tissue from my back pocket and attempted to stay my dripping nose. A teenaged boy, probably from the high school a few blocks away, squatted down beside me. "Are you hurt? Should I call someone?" he asked, his phone in his hand.

"No. It's okay. I'm fine. Really. Thanks, though," I said, wiping my face and pushing myself to my feet. "I'll be fine."

"'K," he said, glancing around. "If you're sure." And he was off.

Even the kids *are nice in Canada,* I thought, blowing my red and sore nose. *Truthfully, I don't want nice – or any – interaction today.* Looking back toward our apartment, I felt the draw of its dim, comforting oblivion. *No,* I thought, with a quick shake of my head. Turning back up the street, I squared my shoulders and continued toward my suffering seedlings.

A few minutes later I rounded the corner of Saint Paul's central building where a patchwork of greens reached for the sun. The previous summer my garden had consisted of five plastic pots of tomatoes balanced on a wire-wrapped pallet in our back parking lot. This spring, three weeks after everyone else had planted, an anonymous neighbour gave up his plot in the community garden behind the university. I was first on the waiting list. Granted, it was the shadiest, most neglected plot, but over the prior month Pierre and I had cleaned it out, turned the soil, and planted dozens of seeds and starts. The last time I'd been here had been four days ago, when I was still smiling.

Pierre, Porter, and I had met Catherine and Zoe here and planted a half-flat of marigolds among the vegetables. We dunked watering cans into the rain barrels, gently sprinkling the rows of new lives. Our walk here had been painstakingly slow, as Porter's pace had become more of a start-stop over the previous weeks; every few feet required a thorough sniffing.

When we arrived at the gardens, and he caught sight of tiny Zoe, he raised up on his toes like a new puppy. Play-bowing and feinting, they romped and ran and rolled in the warm grass together. Catherine, Pierre, and I laughed in amazement, as none of us had seen the old gent do more than mosey or sleep for the past several weeks. Eventually the two had tired and flopped down next to each other – panting and smiling. Our walk back home had been achingly slow. Porter slept until dinner and then again until waking us all with a cry at 1:30 AM. Two hours later at the emergency vet's on a soft pink blanket on the floor, we held him close and I whispered the most difficult "yes" I'd ever had to deliver, approving the final injection. Moments later he flew away from his cancer-ridden body, covered in our tears and taking a huge piece of my heart.

Approaching my plot alone, I found the scarlet runner beans – already almost two feet long – winding their way across the back corner and wilting along with the tomato, marigold and broccoli plants. Multiple patches of tiny grey-green sprouts were pushing up through the dry, light soil. The adjoining beds had become lush with recognizable vegetables and flowers. I opened the rain-barrel gate and pressed faded green watering cans down into the warm, full drums. Walking slowly back and forth, I kept my gaze down, feeling the weight of each footstep, watching the soil turn dark in patches and rows as it absorbed the life-giving water. Again and again I filled and emptied the cans.

On one of my unhurried treks, I glanced at the spot where Porter used to lay, stopped and looked up, and sent him my love. Then I took a long breath and made a choice. After refilling the watering cans, I took the first deliberate steps in the practice of letting Porter go and turned my thoughts on a different course.

College is half-way finished. I have met a few fascinating people in the program – not only fellow students, but also Moira, our Canadian Authors, Editing, and Web Writing teacher. We met a number of times for tea or lunch last semester and, after establishing a Cone of Silence, often discussed the tribulations and struggles of both attending and teaching college. Those conversations helped me realize that I wouldn't be striving to become a college teacher. I felt for her, though, and listened to the difficulties as well as toasting to the positive aspects of her classes. Of our half dozen instructors, she was by far my favourite and the one from whom I was learning the most. In addition, Porter became play-buddies with her landlord's bear-sized golden retriever. Her sleek white cat, Tundra, won't miss our visits, but Hudson certainly will.

From the far side of Saint Paul U's commons building I hear yipping and a deep, rumbling bark as people's pups run and play in the huge fields along the river. A Rottweiler pulled his owner past the gardens, heading toward the din. I set the nearly-empty watering cans down and watched the young man grapple with the leash, finally releasing his dog and dashing after him around the corner. I stretched up and flowed forward into a yoga sun salutation, savouring the stretch through my shoulders and low back. Picking up the cans on my way back to standing, I wend my way back to my thoughts and the rain barrels.

Early last semester, I discovered another great learning resource – again, on the Internet – the *CanadaVisa Immigration Forum.* My first discovery was exciting news. International students are eligible to work, provided the jobs are on campus. The following week I signed up to be a peer tutor. It was the lowest paying job I had had since university days, but I loved the work. My appointments quickly filled with a wide variety of students, from kids with Asperger's Syndrome to those who were baffled by grammar or just needed support with their essays. By far my most prized students, though, were the ones who spoke English as a new language. I now had acquaintances (and in some cases, even friends) from Korea, Argentina, Thailand, Iran, South Africa, China, Yemen, India, Guatemala, Nepal, Saudi Arabia, and Japan. Every one blessed me by throwing open windows into cultures I had never explored; I could feel my world expanding.

Back in my garden, the plastic watering can gurgled as it emptied onto the 10-by-20-foot patch of rich Canadian soil. Already the beefsteak, roma, and cherry tomato plants – the first to be watered – were beginning to perk up. I returned the cans to the shed and dug into the bottom of the tool bin, choosing a handful of weathered bamboo poles and some soft Velcro ties. It was time to tie the runner beans up to a teepee, to get them started on their right path. Pressing the poles deep into the dirt and binding their tops securely, my thoughts again wandered back to school.

The Professional Writing program has been hectic, with courses ranging from research and editing to storytelling, government writing, and even some graphic design. Overlapping assignments, mid-terms, and the first two semester's finals raised my blood pressure, as I put more effort into earning high marks than I ever did in university. Finding and hiring three different pet-sitters and then transporting Porter to and from their homes added to the stress, until Lulu and Mark moved in upstairs and his daily commute became a short, though sometimes arduous two-story climb.

Because of the international tuition costs, not only have I wanted Pierre to feel appreciated for spending so much money to keep me here, I also want him to be proud of me. When the final marks arrived in December and April, I was astonished to find that I had earned A-pluses or A's in every class – both semesters. Pierre was so cute about it. Sitting back with a smug smile on his face, as if to say, *See? I told you so!,* he grabbed me up and asked where he could take me to dinner. Our celebratory kisses turned to caresses, and – oh well, dinner had to wait.

Winding and tying up the final bean sprout, I felt a fragile smile on my face, the first glimmer of happiness returning as the sun beat down on my shoulders. I dropped the remaining ties back into the tool bin and spun the lock just as two other gardeners rode up on their bikes. A young black lab panting around a wet tennis ball loped between them.

"Hey there," the freckled, pink-faced girl called across to me, as she climbed off her bicycle. "Gorgeous day, eh?" Her dog wound his way along the paths, obviously well trained in the ways of garden beds. He dropped the soggy yellow ball at my feet and pranced away, glancing down and then up into my eyes, over and over, his tail wagging delightedly.

"It is, indeed," I said with a smile, and stooped to pick up the ball.

Chapter 13
December 2010   Six months later

"Wanna stop for a beer?" Dana asked. At twenty-one, she was less than half my age, a difference that – at least most of the time – seemed inconsequential. We had joked, as wordsmiths often do, when the college came up with a euphemism for me. It seemed I was now a Mature Student; *Ha!* we quipped, *How could the administration know that I don't howl at fart jokes or amuse my friends by sticking pencils up my nose?*

Luckily, my spreading wrinkles and that sophisticated title didn't stop most of the classmates from including me in activities, either in or outside the classrooms. Our first weeks had been almost unbearably awkward. Tongue-tied and fidgeting, we were forty-three introverted wanna-be writers, who found our way to various classrooms throughout the maze-like campus. Over the months, we forged friendships and watched almost half of the disgruntled or floundering students disappear.

Dana and I were two of the twenty-six remaining. Bright and comical, with a talent for writing and depth of thought that astonished me, Dana let down her protective class-clown shield when it was just the two of us, a subtle shift that felt like such an honour. Her roly-poly pug, Biggie – regularly teased for his homely countenance and protruding tongue, especially by Dana herself – had been one of Porter's pals. Our pups had become the inspiration for one of my most challenging assignments, the children's story in Creative Writing, a tale I'd been unable to read since Porter's passing in June.

Dana's red-brick high-rise apartment was on my route to the college, so on occasion she skipped her usual bus commute and rode with me. It was a win for both of us. She didn't have to stand in the cold waiting to sit next to who-knows-who, and I got to enjoy her lighthearted company. Thursday evening chauffeur rides had become almost a ritual and bellying up to a glossy varnished high bar-table or – weather permitting – soaking in the sun at an outdoor patio table, often turned into a three-hour stress-relief session, a laughter-filled party for two new friends.

"I'd love to have a beer," I answered, turning the car down Merivale. "Our usual spot?"

"Absolutely."

Montana's, a chain restaurant sitting on a busy thoroughfare, with its rustic old-west décor and chatty staff, had become a favourite hangout over the previous year. Pierre loved their barbequed ribs, and now and then, he and Dana's partner, Eliot, would join us for dinner after our girls-only happy hour. I knew that this time we'd make it a relatively short stop, though. It was the end of third semester, and on the drive between the college and the pub, we discussed two final quizzes, the 5000-word feature stories, and our assigned news reports, all due before Christmas break.

Shrugging out of our bulky coats, we waved to the bartender, Emily, who greeted us with her wide, welcoming smile. "Pitcher of Canadian?" she asked once she made her way to our table.

"Just a couple of pints this time," I said, confirming with Dana.

"Sounds good."

Dana and I chatted about the upcoming holidays and her and Eliot's train trip home to Barrie. It sounded as though their celebrations would be busy and rambunctious, and her parents' home would be crowded, once again, with people and laughter. Pictures of my family's Christmas Eve rituals washed through my mind, and a sharp twinge of sadness pinched my Adam's apple. *When*, I wondered, *would we ever go back to Washington for the holiday celebrations?* Pressing my fingers to my throat, I shook myself back to the pub, only to see Dana looking at me in confusion.

"Sorry… spaced off there. What were you saying?"

"I asked what's the latest with the house," she said, smiling as Emily delivered our beers.

"It's supposed to close next Friday," I said, holding up crossed fingers. She mirrored my gesture. "We still have some packing to do, but the apartment's rent is covered until the first of the year, so there's no panic. Do you feel like sticking around and helping us paint bedrooms during Christmas week?" We both laughed and toasted to that silly idea.

In mid-October, Pierre had discovered a stone-front rambler in Bells Corners on Ottawa's multiple listing site. With an asking price significantly higher than our top figure, I automatically brushed it off. As I had told many real estate clients, it is unwise to even walk through homes outside of your price range. Why torture yourself with something you can't have?

We had been shopping online for months by that point, poring over the MLS listings, discussing the pros and cons of different areas. We'd driven through neighbourhoods all over the city, though none that far west of city centre, and had toured a number of homes. The photos of the Dorland house captivated us, and Pierre persuaded me to just "pop in and see." Against my internal-real-estate-agent's better judgment, we visited its first open house on a glowing autumn Sunday afternoon.

There were so many things right about it: the terra-cotta coloured living room walls, shown off by floor-to-ceiling windows; the knotty pine kitchen cupboards just like Gramps and Gran's; the spacious shop in a newly-finished basement with an on-demand hot water heater; multiple garden beds and evergreen trees. It sat in a quiet development named *Lynwood Village,* a different spelling, but the same as my previous neighbourhood in north Seattle. Everything felt so inviting. Even the agent holding the open house was a smiling, soft-spoken young man with a captivating Hispanic accent. We kept a close eye on the MLS and talked about the place numerous times over the next few weeks. The day after we walked through it a second time, the sellers dropped the price $30,000. Pierre immediately called his high school friend, a prominent Keller Williams Realtor®, and put in an offer. Two tense days later, we had a signed-around agreement.

"We're hoping to throw a Christmas party, though we may still be surrounded by boxes," I said. "I'm sad that you and Eliot will be gone, but it sounds as though some of our classmates are staying in town."

"Yeah, there are sure to be some. And you'll have to have a housewarming once we're back," Dana said.

"You got it! Oh. And… we just learned that this will be a Gotcha Party, too."

"*Whaaaat?*"

"We've only told a couple of people, but we applied to adopt a rescued golden retriever named Copper from upstate New York. The acceptance email arrived this morning. We're driving down to Dunkirk the week after next to pick him up. My online golden group calls that the Gotcha Day!"

Halfway through the telling, Dana nearly jumped off her chair. "Oh my *god!* That is so awesome!! Do you have pictures?"

I pulled out my phone and showed her the photos that his rescuer had posted on PetFinder. Copper was an apt name for the big, red, curly-haired dog. He looked a little goofy, with droopy eyes, a big smile, and three black spots on his lolling tongue. "One of my golden-owning pals calls those 'place-treats-here spots,'" I said, when she asked whether he was part Chow. "They're actually pretty common in purebred gold dogs."

"Why would someone give up this gorgeous boy?" Dana asked, flipping back and forth between the photos.

"Believe it or not, the poor guy lived most of his seven-and-a-half years in an outdoor pen, in the extreme weather outside Buffalo. His owner was ill, and the outdoor-dog rescue group finally convinced her to give him and his kennel-mates up."

"No! What an awful life!" she said, lifting her glass. "Well, he doesn't know it yet, but he just won the jackpot. I can't wait to hug him and for him to meet Biggie."

Sipping our beers, we scrolled on, looking through older photos, including some of Porter and Biggie frolicking through the grass and mud puddles at Saint Paul University. Dana hadn't seen the shots of the afternoon we had scattered his ashes, so we perused those slowly, both of us tearing up.

"He was a sweet old gentleman," she said, gazing at a close-up of his soulful eyes and heart-shaped white face. "I'm sure he would approve."

"Yeah, they'd probably have been great friends if he were still here," I said. "Now we just have to hope that he and Penny get along. The foster family says he mostly ignores their cats."

"*Copper* and *Penny?* Really, Patrice? Did you plan that?"

"Swear to god, Dana. They came to us with those names. I'm taking it as a positive omen."

A couple of weeks after Porter's death left a ragged hole in our hearts and our family, I began searching Kijiji's *Available Pets* section. I wasn't ready for another dog right away, but the apartment felt barren to me without a fuzzy beast to coddle and care for. Pierre and

I discussed it at length. He had never lived with a cat, but I had an inkling that he would feel a kinship with their autonomous natures. We first decided that kitten energy was a bit too much at our age. My top choice would have been a bonded pair of youngsters. However, the only two-cat listing was for a pair of overweight, long-haired felines who weren't completely litter-box reliable. As sad as they looked, I could just imagine Pierre's reaction to surprise puddles; honestly, neither of us would have handled that well, but I had a feeling Pierre would become a cat-hater long before I could get them trained.

Penny was the third young cat we met. Pulling up to her owner's apartment in the east-end Vanier district, we saw her chasing small blue butterflies in the front yard. She was slight and had distinct tri-colour calico/tortoiseshell markings along with some subtle tabby stripes, a torbie, her paperwork said. When Pierre walked toward them, and she turned her curious puss-face to him, I swear I saw him melt. He knew. Immediately. After a short half-French/half-English conversation with her owner – guaranteeing that if we didn't think she was the best cat ever, he'd take her back – we were both sold. Penny yowled her way across town to her new home with us. Car rides were not her thing.

We learned the hard way that, although she loved people, other cats were on her most-despised list. A six-week hissing/growling, separate-room, cat-sitting experiment clearly illustrated that no… she would not be getting a new feline sister or brother anytime soon… or *ever*, if she had a say. But what about a dog? Before applying to adopt Copper, we borrowed the upstairs neighbour's gold dog for an evening, to be sure she wouldn't go ballistic. After an initial puffball imitation and dash to the top of her cat stand, Penny turned her back, yawned and curled up for a nap. Ten minutes later she snuck down, crept up on the snoozing Reuben, stretched close for a few sniffs, turned up her nose, and sauntered away. I figured we were probably safe.

Our glasses empty, Dana and I talked each other out of a refill and paid the bill. As we stepped through the heavy front doors into a blast of swirling wet snow, I looked up the street and wondered whether I would be here to celebrate the following Christmas with Pierre and my new, growing group of friends.

"Danes…," I started, loath to bring up bad news, but the words poured out in spite of my aversion. "We haven't heard back from Pierre's soon-to-be ex yet."

"Aww, shit," she said, as we slogged out to the parking lot. "What is *keeping* that woman?"

"Well, she might be punishing us, knowing it's impossible for us to get married as long as their divorce is pending. Pierre says she's not a mean-spirited person, though, so, that doesn't quite make sense. I'm thinking she's just scared. There's really no way for us to know, since they do not speak. Neither of their lawyers seem to be in any rush, which is making me crazy. Of course, I can't call them to light a spark, but there are only seven months left on my student permit, which Pierre's lawyer knows. I *think* we have enough time to get married and apply for my Permanent Residency before then, but only if the divorce happens soon."

Dana swiped her sleeve across the top of the passenger door and climbed into the car, and I slipped around the outside, using a telescoping brush to sweep the heavy mat of snow off the hood, roof, and windows.

When I got in, she said, "What happens if it doesn't? Go through, that is."

"Hopefully, I could get another visitor's permit until it does. If they won't grant me one, we've talked about getting me a room or apartment just across the border for a while."

"Oh man!" she said, lifting and then dropping her mittened hands into her lap.

"We'll do whatever it takes," I said. "I'm still looking for alternatives, but so far, this is all we've got." Maneuvering behind the mall and twisting through Dana's neighbourhood, we pulled up to her apartment building and hugged our see-you-tomorrows.

The remainder of my drive home was a picturesque one along urban Meadowlands Avenue to Hogs Back Park and Falls, and then winding up Colonel By Drive along the dark, mostly-drained-but-not-yet-frozen canal. I would miss this drive once we moved. Even when it was a mucky mess like it was now, the majestic homes, mature trees and park that lined the canal created a sense of quiet serenity in the midst of the busy city.

Sliding into my parking space behind our apartment and shutting off the car, I let myself sit in the silent stillness for a moment and watched as mammoth snowflakes shrouded my view of the neighbours' warmly-lit windows. From under my whirlwind thoughts of upcoming activities crept the incessant unease, the concern that I worked every day to pray away. Regardless of all the steps we had taken so far and the optimistic plans we were making, we still didn't know how – or even whether – I could stay.

Chapter 14

March 2011   Three months later

"Thank you, Sangita. I'll see you again next
Tuesday," I said, standing up from our round
wooden table in the college library.

"Thank you, Patrice," came her soft, Nepali-
accented reply. She carefully gathered her laptop and
class notes, swung her daughter's cast-off lavender
backpack over her shoulder and headed through the
noisy work-space and out the exit. It was our fifth
tutoring appointment and it seemed as though her
shyness was finally beginning to abate. Hers was a
familiar pattern. Often immigrant students were
tentative about speaking the new language.
Embarrassment about mispronunciation or misuse of
words and fear of being laughed at caused many,
including Sangita, to hide in the back of classrooms,
rarely participating. She was beginning to open up with
me. Soon, I hoped she would also begin to voluntarily
share her thoughts in her classes.

I settled back into the squeaky blue chair and
glanced again at the calendar page in my notebook.
Hmm. An hour to kill before Edward's appointment. Think I'll

ask whether the disabled study cubicle is already reserved. It had only taken a couple of appointments to discover that Edward, one of my three tutoring students with Asperger's, was repeatedly distracted and overwhelmed by the busy library environment.

We had tried one session in the Centre for Students with Disabilities on the main floor. Even in that relatively quiet, computer-lined room, the comings and goings of other students disrupted his flow, often requiring a restart of the lesson. Edward's counselor suggested we try meeting in one of the open-ceilinged, two-person study closets tucked into a corner of the library. It was a brilliant solution, one which I now used with all three of the students with Asperger's. Disabled students had first claim to the private rooms. However, the librarians were completely fine with non-disabled students reserving them, with the caveat that we could be scooted out at any time. With that in mind, I approached the check-out counter.

Moments later, I slid closed the cube's clouded door, pulled out my binders and pens, and sat down in front of the yellow, oversized keyboard. *What to do?* Sighing, I opened my college Outlook account and found a dozen new emails. The first was an update from our program coordinator reminding us all to confirm that we had met with our placement mentors. I had and couldn't wait to start the final piece of the program, a full-time, seven-week placement at the Peace and Environment Resource Centre which began the week after next.

As I was skimming through the list of emails, the one I'd been waiting for popped in from the International Education Centre, three floors above the library. It turned out that a cancelled appointment made it possible for me to meet with Michelle in – I glanced at the corner of the screen – ten minutes. What luck! Knowing how busy her schedule was, I shot off a quick confirmation, repacked my briefcase, and scribbled a note to Edward, on the off-chance that the meeting with Michelle ran long. Then, I headed up the central building's familiar crowded stairs.

I remembered the first time I took this staircase to our initial meeting, two years before. There had been a long line snaking into the International Education Centre. For half an hour we edged forward as I marveled at the variety of languages people spoke. Once inside, the receptionist pointed me into head advisor Michelle Cameron's tiny but warm office. Behind the desk sat a softly smiling, neatly dressed woman in her early thirties. She immediately stood to shake my hand, enveloping it in both of hers. "Welcome to Canada and Algonquin College," she had said in a calm, compassionate voice. "How can I make your life here easier?"

Sometimes, I thought now, trekking up the clear painted cement steps, *a position is filled by exactly the right person.* From that first greeting, I'd decided to be candid and share my true reason for attending the college. After hearing my story, she had again reached across her desk without hesitation and clasped my hand. "People come to college for all kinds of reasons, Patrice," she said. "If yours is to allow you to stay with your true love, I'm totally with you. Please never hesitate to contact me if you think I can help." Her patience, kindness, and seemingly photographic memory always left me feeling that no matter what struggle arose, with her support, we would overcome it.

Although it had been months since we'd last met, her first question was, "So, are wedding congratulations in order?"

To my chagrin, tears welled up in my eyes. "Not yet, I'm afraid," I said, swallowing back the lump in my throat. "We keep hoping to hear from the divorce lawyer, but nothing yet, and time is running out. My study permit expires in less than four months. I had hoped to have my Permanent Residency application in by now with Pierre as my spousal sponsor, but so far, that's been impossible."

Nodding her head, she shifted her gaze and tapped a few keys on her computer's keyboard. "Well, it sounds as though you're going to have to go with Plan B."

"There's a *Plan B*?" I said, my jaw dropping and brows practically lifting to my hairline.

"Yes ma'am," she smiled. "You are in a two-year certificate program, correct?" I nodded. "Well, Citizenship and Immigration offers a post-graduate work permit for higher education international grads. It takes a while to process, but you can apply for a three-year work permit after your two-year certification."

"*You are kidding me?!* I have spent so many hours on the CIC site; why have I never seen this information?" It was all I could do to not spin the monitor around on her huge desk, so I could see the page.

"It's a few levels deep in the immigration site," Michelle said, as she emailed me the information and links.

"Maybe they don't want to encourage people to go that route?" I said.

"Perhaps not," she said, her brow furrowing as she continued clicking and skimming. "It seems quite odd. You'd think the government would want to *keep* graduates of Canadian colleges and universities rather than send them back home, wouldn't you?"

"Yeah, that would make sense. Very strange… But let me get this straight. You're saying that once I graduate, I can stay and work *legally* for *three more years??*"

"That's right," she said, turning her deep blue eyes back to me. Glancing again at the screen, she continued, "Unfortunately though, it looks like we're too close to your study permit's expiry date to apply now…aaand… you don't yet have your certificate."

All of the air drained out of my chest.

She typed some more. "However, …" I held onto the seat of my chair. "You *might* be able to apply for a study permit *extension* and *then* apply for the post-grad work permit once your certificate arrives…. Yes. Yes, I think this will work! That should give you some wiggle room!"

"Will they approve an extension if I'm not continuing my studies?"

She nodded, "They should, since you'll soon be applying for the work permit."

"What reason do I give?"

"Tell them the truth; just keep it simple, and only request three months or so," she said. "Of course, you'll have to prove again that you have sufficient funds to support yourself and pay for your return to the States. And whatever you do, don't do anything illegal; even a DUI would be grounds for permanent deportation. As long as you comply with the visa requirements and don't let anything expire while you're here, you should be just fine."

I practically floated back down to the library. Fortunately, a few minutes remained before Edward's appointment, so I sat in meditation in the cubicle until he arrived. Again, it came to me that supporting students with learning disabilities helped bring my own struggles into perspective. I felt such compassion for their constant challenges and realized that, although this immigration process was stressful, in general, my life was overflowing with blessings. An hour of intense concentration later, Edward and I left the cube together and said our quick goodbyes as he headed to the bus stop and I turned toward the parking lot.

Once home, I followed the links Michelle had sent and read all I could find on the post-graduate work permit. There it was. Incredibly, it had been there all along, the key to my next immigration step. I was a half hour and three pages into my online application for the study permit extension when I heard Pierre's car pull into the drive. Jumping up from the couch, Copper, Penny and I met him halfway up the walkway.

"Three more years!" I cried, wrapping him into a huge bear hug. "It looks as though the college is going to give me three more years!"

Chapter 15

June 2012 Nine months later

Eight of us, clad in white dress shirts and black vests, slacks, and shoes, sat forward on sagging red leather couches in the Green Room. We each held a thick, stapled crew script in our lap. Opening night had arrived, and the first of three weeks of performances began in under an hour. We could hear the cast members chanting from the dressing rooms across the hall, "Fee fee fee fee, fah fah fah fah, fub fub fub fub, gee gee gee gee, gah gah gah gah, gub gub gub gub, hee hee hee hee...." In full 18th-century costumes, hair, and makeup, they warmed up their voices while we read our nineteen scene changes aloud.

Each set-crew member had rehearsed a furniture-moving role (or two) over the previous two weeks while the set was built. Now it was a matter of executing the moves flawlessly, turning and rearranging a central rotating door; three-panel dividers; tables and chairs; a giant, unwieldy wall; a back-breaking round pouffe; a chaise, bench, and bed.

Our goals were to change the Marquise's salon to Madame de Tourvel's, Madame de Rosemonde's and one of five other sets, each in under a minute. Six of us poured out from either side of backstage in what was called *brown light*, the near-darkness tinting our hands and faces an eerie blue. Val, our stage right Crew Chief, listened on headset to the stage manager and, at the end of each scene as the lights went down, cued us with a whispered, "GO!" Lifting and spinning, we squinted, locating moon, star, and angle-cut pieces of tape on the black painted stage.

Quickly but silently we set ornate furniture in their precise positions: chaise legs on stars, tables on moons. From above on the catwalk, our "flyer" lowered/flew in and raised/flew out an array of velvet curtains and windows attached to thick, weighted cables.

The potential for on-stage collisions with exiting actors or between moving set pieces was colossal. When it worked according to Geoff, our director's vision, we performed brief, incredibly graceful dances. Like devoted servants, at the end of each change, we bowed before slipping back between the heavy dust-scented curtains that hid us from the audience. This was far from the typically boring between-scenes set changes and, especially because of the large number of them, added a beauty and depth to the performance rarely seen.

With butterflies in my stomach, I read out my next move: "Enter downstage left, move Chair 1, clear

Chaise with H1, exit upstage right." I envisioned the charged glow-tape spike marks on the stage floor and raised my eyebrows at Pierre. He would be at the head of the chaise lounge that we moved offstage during that change. It was comforting to know that we would perform many of our moves together. Nothing seemed to faze him. I thought back briefly to our arrival a half hour earlier. Stopping on the way in, we had posed for photos beside the marquee in front of the Ottawa Little Theatre.

"NOW SHOWING," it proclaimed, "Dangerous Liaisons, June 5 – 23, 2012. Curtain at 8:00 PM."

Tonight was my first time in front of an audience… unless you counted my kindergarten performance as Baby Billy Goat Gruff. Way back then, I froze half-way across the bridge, completely forgetting my one line, far more terrified of the watching parents than the troll below. Those titters at the darling little paralyzed towhead stayed with me for years. While my high school friends raved about the fun they had in drama classes, I broke out in a sweat at the thought and avoided any hint of a spotlight. Until now. All because of Val. Looking across at her, the memory of our meeting backstage a few months earlier flowed through my mind.

Pierre and I rarely returned to Second Life once we were together in real life and I began meeting college friends. One day, however, I decided to pop in to see whether there were any local people in that virtual world. Sure enough, there was a very small group called SLers of Ottawa. To my surprise, the group's creator lived only a few blocks from our apartment. Meeting for a beer at the neighbourhood Royal Oak overlooking the canal, he invited us to attend an upcoming Ottawa Little Theatre play, in which he had a small part. It had been years since either Pierre or I had attended a stage performance, and all had been big-budget professional shows. The Ottawa Little Theatre, preparing for its 100th season celebration, was a community playhouse with a handful of paid staff; all others, including the cast and crew of every show, were volunteers.

"I'd like to introduce you to my friend, Val," he told us. "I think you'll really love her."

Later that month, our hands red and tingling from clapping, he did introduce us to Val. Greeting us with warm, vivacious hugs, she took us on a grand backstage tour and talked us into staying for a drink at that evening's Green Room bash. From that very first hug, we discussed later, we recognized each other as kindred souls, sisters from different mothers. Since then, we had spent hours together, laughing over shared stories, walking, and confirming our initial impression. Her primary activity over the past 25 years – aside from her government job – was volunteering at the OLT so we talked about the theatre a *lot*.

"Come give it a try," she said, almost from that first night. "We would love to have you! What sounds interesting? Sound? Lighting? Costumes? Or maybe you'd like to work either set or props with me…." The hook was set when she told us that *Dangerous Liaisons* (a story Pierre and I both knew and loved) was on the bill. We talked it over and signed on. And here we were, on opening night!

Jenn, our flyer, gave me a nudge. Looking back down at my script and diagram, I read out, "Enter upstage left, set divider, clear needlepoint from chaise, exit upstage left."

Dong, dung, ding. The soft rising tones of the bell calling the audience to their seats rang through the Green Room speakers, followed by Jim, our stage manager's voice, "That's ten minutes 'til showtime, folks. Ten minutes 'til showtime. May we have Act I beginners, please. Act I beginners. Break legs, everyone." Making the decision to keep my thoughts on the script and pretend the house was empty, I stood with the rest of the team and wound my way up the stairs to the humming, crowded wings.

A little over two hours later, we all skipped down and packed into the Green Room, reveling in the standing ovation and everyone's near-perfect performances. The centre of the room held tables laden with delicious-smelling food: simmering meatballs, cheesy casseroles, pasta and potato salads. A side table was crammed with glasses and bottles of wine, liquor, and beer. Hospitality volunteers had set out at least a dozen giant bouquets in vases. The cast and crew, our guests, and theatre regulars mingled; the volume of our exuberant voices and laughter was deafening. Everyone hugged everyone. People, many becoming familiar after the prior weeks' rehearsals, hugged us or shook our hands saying, "Congratulations!" "Bravo!" "Wonderful show!" again and again. Val pulled us both in, and then, looking out over the room, raised her drink to ours.

The three of us touched glasses as she shouted over the din through her contagious smile, "Welcome to the family!"

What seemed like an hour later, but was actually four, Pierre and I were deep in conversation with Jim, the stage manager, hearing the story of the theatre's mischievous resident ghost, Martha. At the far end of the room, Val bid two of the cast members goodnight, then wove her way between friends and settled in beside me on the couch. "Having fun?" she asked, easily guessing the answer.

"Having a blast," I said, throwing my arm across her shoulder.

"Awesome!" she said, "You two jumped right in to probably the most intense crew show I've ever worked, and you're totally rockin' it. So… no need to answer right now… but in a couple of months we'll be holding auditions for *Pride and Prejudice*. Geoff's directing again, and I'll be Assistant Director. How would you and Pierre feel about possibly being co-Crew Chiefs?"

Looking around the room, still three-quarters full of creative, partying people at 2:00 A.M., I turned back to her with a grin. "We're huge Jane Austin fans! Let's talk about what chiefing entails," I said. "Sounds scary and delightful. No promises, but can P&P really say *no* to working *P&P*?"

Chapter 16

November 2012   Five months later

Fidgeting on the front edge of a folding chair behind the stage left props table, I felt the warmth of Pierre's hand rub across and then settle between my shoulder blades. Val disappeared behind the upstage scrim with a grin and a wave. *Yes… I can see how this could become addictive.*

Preset for *The Hollow* was finished; now we could relax for forty-five minutes until our moves at intermission. Pierre, bored with this somewhat banal role, pulled out his cell phone and opened his favourite meditation program, some sort of complex solitaire game that he enjoyed and regularly won, but that made no sense to me.

In three minutes, the house doors would open, and the audience would pour in. At this point, all we knew of them was the muffled hubbub which filled the lobby. Soon, the four hundred and sixty red velvet seats would become a multi-coloured sea of murmuring, expectant patrons. Because most of the Ottawa Little Theatre's subscribers were retirement-aged and older, Agatha Christie shows nearly always sold out. And today was no exception. Grabbing my props script, I hopped up once more and hustled back out on stage for a final look, checking off each item.

Martini, sherry, and rocks glasses were lined up perfectly on the drinks table in front of three crystal decanters filled mostly full of water posing as gin and two strengths of tea as brandy and whiskey. Newspapers were folded and set *just so* on the hassock and next to the light bulb-and-cellophane lit fireplace. Chocolate covered raisins were tucked into a special box on the end table. A variety of modeling clay pieces, soon to be snatched up by the actress playing Henrietta, were placed strategically just out of view beyond open French doors. The list filled the remainder of the page. Check, check, check. Everything was set.

Pierre was on his feet murmuring with a couple of the actors when I stepped back into the wings. *Sotto voce* we encouraged the cast to "break legs" and then slipped through the heavy backstage door leading down to the Green Room. Two of the actors whose characters weren't on until the third scene were running lines for their upcoming shows. Otherwise, the long, couch-lined room was deserted. A donated large-screen TV fuzzily broadcast the dimly-lit stage upstairs, the heads of front row patrons rising as the audience stood to sing "O Canada"; a long-held tradition, the anthem was sung before every performance. Many in the audience sang the original French version, the two languages flowing together in harmony. It was upstairs in the wings that I learned its hopeful lyrics. … *God keep our land glorious and free. O Canada, we stand on guard for thee.* Finally, the audience settled into their seats as the theatre went dark for the opening act.

Since tomorrow was closing night of this three-week run, we no longer watched the entire play, but kept an ear cocked, knowing the dialogue that ended Act One. Meanwhile, we were free. Snuggling up on a couch, we reminisced over the previous month.

Val had said that Jane and Marti, the props designers for *The Hollow*, just need another couple hands to spell them one or two nights a week. "Setting up and moving props for this show will be a *breeze*," she'd said, and she was right. It was, in fact, so easy, that one of us could have covered it, except that would have meant long evenings apart. So, we both came and helped out, sitting backstage or in the Green Room for stretches, Pierre playing online cards and me perusing Facebook, reading articles, or checking emails.

"Have I mentioned that I'd rather not do props again?" he asked for the third time.

"Yes, honey. I get it. Props are not your thing. We've got a break from theatre, then we will be back on set crew in a few months for *Pride and Prejudice*… if you're still up for it," I said, hoping I hadn't lost my backstage partner.

"Oh yeah. That I'm definitely looking forward to," he said, squeezing my hand. Then he reached for his cellphone and we fell into our comfortable routine, the lines of the play softly coming through the speaker in the background.

Opening Outlook, the number 2738 popped up from the bottom of the screen, 2 unread. *Good grief!* I realized that it had been months since I had cleaned out my inbox, so scrolling down, I began the process of deleting and organizing.

Most of the emails I highlighted and slid straight into the trash bin. I created and filled three new sub-folders under "Algonquin College": *Short Stories, Grammar for Writers,* and *Life Writing.* These three online courses I'd taken over the past year had acted as my safety raft, keeping my tutoring eligibility current so I could continue working on campus, and keeping my mind busy with structured study.

Opening and perusing a few of the emails from the *Short Stories* folder helped me remember how much I preferred practical courses to theory. The weekly emailed lessons were packed with typed lectures on point-of-view, character, setting, style, and conflict. My journal entries on each subject had been submitted, but in the entire semester, we'd only written and revised one short story. I reminded myself *Not all courses are for you,* mentally sent the instructor my best wishes, and closed the folder.

The presentation of the *Grammar for Writers* course held last winter had been a bit of a yawner, but the material and course notes were invaluable. Its folder absorbed dozens of emails; each week's lectures broken into mini-sessions on everything from adjectives to semi-colons, prepositions, and proper verb tense. There were quizzes, practice tests, and copies of the mid-term and final exams. It felt like a feast of information for my inner English-tutor nerd's palate. Dry as they might be, these were keepers, for sure.

From the static-filled TV speaker, we heard Lucy, Edward, Lady Angkatell, and Gerda's lines as they approached the culmination of Act One. Pierre looked up from his game and simultaneously we clicked off our phones and stood to go. Passing the cast in the stairwell, we smiled at their chatter, hearing snippets of conversation about the lively audience, a skipped line, and John's excellent death scene. Seemingly, Act One was a hit.

Pierre worked his way up from the bottom of the props list and I started at the top, checking as we removed fake cigarettes, handbags, and sweaters, and placed flowers, knitting and bread-and-butter sandwiches for the second act. Washing drinks glasses, replacing them, and closing all stage doors were our final moves during the twenty-minute intermission. In another hour, we would return to wash dishes again and gather the four plastic guns for Jim to lock up for the night; this was Canada, and – props or not – firearms were treated with an intense and sober respect.

And then it would be time for the crew night party. Hosted by the cast, the crew teams, from the director and his assistants to set, lights and sound, costumes, makeup, and props would be recognized and given small appreciation gifts. But in the meantime, "May I have Act Two beginners please; Act Two beginners," Jim spoke into the mic to the Green and dressing rooms, and we headed back down the stairs.

After making myself a cup of ginger tea – the mint tin, which I regularly refilled was empty again – I resumed my seat on the leather couch next to Pierre and dug my phone back out of my purse.

"What are you up to there, sweetheart?"

"Clearing out my inbox," I said, logging back into my account. "It was getting pretty out of control."

"Oooh. Fun," he laughed. "I'll leave you to it."

Where was I? Ah, yes. Last fall's emails from the *Life Writing* class. Clicking through them one at a time I found myself re-reading portions of Kathryn, the instructor's clear and cohesive lessons. *What an excellent teacher! Perhaps one day I'll take another of her classes.* This one was all about creative non-fiction, using our story-telling skills to bring true stories to life. The course had been full – more than thirty students from all around Ontario had signed up, logged in, and submitted assignments both privately to her and publicly to the entire class.

There in my inbox were three stories I had saved from Bernice, my favourite fellow student. Her Week 1 introduction had caught my attention, not only for the depth and flow of her writing style, but also for the subject matter about which she planned to write. She had grown up with a brother whose difficult birth had left him with brain damage. From her first story, I could feel her love for him, and it was clear that her life had been one of challenge and deep exploration. Hers were the pieces I looked for every week, and I was thrilled to find that she often commented on mine, as well. I learned that she lived in a suburb on the far side of Toronto, unfortunately a six-hour drive from home. *I wonder how she is doing now and whether she is still writing.* Dragging the last of the *Life Writing* emailed lessons into their folder, I continued my chore.

Delete, delete, drag and drop. Post-grad work permit and study permit extension emails went into their respective folders under Immigration. And finally, the inbox was clean. Glancing up at the television screen, I saw that the show was nearly finished. Beside me, Pierre was visiting with Chris, aka dead-John, and the hospitality team was setting up tables and pulling dishes from the fridge, slicing cheese and veggies, and heating up frozen pizzas. I stood at the doorway of the tiny, jam-packed kitchen and asked for a hot-water refill.

Bzzzz. I lifted my phone again and saw a single new email in the inbox. Squinting my eyes and feeling my jaw start to drop, I read the name again. It was from Bernice. *No way.* Sinking back down onto the couch, I opened the email and slowly read it through, blinking back tears. Turning to me, Pierre leaned in asking, "Honey? Is everything okay?"

I felt my heart pounding in my chest. "An email arrived a moment ago from someone I was *just* thinking about," I said, pressing my hand over my heart. "Remember Bernice, the classmate whose stories I read to you – the ones about life with her special-needs brother?"

"Yeah…. Are they all right?"

"Yes. They're both fine. Better than fine, actually. She just sent me an incredible invitation. It seems she and our class instructor are starting an online writing group and they would like me to be a partner!" I felt a sob threatening to bubble up. "*This* is the reason the

Pro Writing group didn't happen. This is the 'something better' I have been praying for!"

Scooting over against me, he wrapped me up into a huge bear hug. "Congratulations, sweetie. You totally deserve this."

Across the room, applause poured from the TV as the lights came back up on the line of actors holding hands and taking their bows. And then, sighing with elation, we watched as the audience rose to its feet.

Chapter 17

February 2013   Three months later

From: Patrice Elston
Date: Thursday, February 21, 2013, 10:47 PM
To: Shelley A
Subject: Re: Catching Up

Dear Shelley,

Thank you so much for your wonderful email letting me know how your life is going and the latest happenings with the Center for Spiritual Living. It sounds as though you are blossoming with your travel writing, and I am thrilled that your retreat cabin is consistently occupied with responsible, vacationing tenants! The reviews on your website make it sound like a heavenly getaway, indeed.

I want to thank you again for facilitating the CSL Connection Circles over the past few years. Your skills and creative questions helped me (and it seemed all the other members) discover a deeper understanding of our truth and consistently *live* our spiritual practice. You are such a gift! Maintaining connection with our community there truly helped me stay grounded and gave me a safe base from which to fly here in Ottawa. I've missed the group over this past year and am so happy that you would like to continue our friendship and share our adventures!

My past year, too, has been full of learning and change, yet a few important things remain the same. (Don't you just love this life?) Yes, I am still with Pierre, and our relationship continues to be the partnership I had dreamed it would be. We are *not* married yet, as we're still waiting for his ex to move forward with their divorce. Their separation contract is firmly in place, and he sends her monthly cheques, but all requests to her lawyer are met with silence, so, my residency here continues to feel somewhat nebulous.

My current "visa" is a post-graduate work permit, which expires in August 2014, giving us a year and a half to marry and get my Permanent Residence (comparable to a U.S. Green Card.) Processing time for PR, though, is currently six to eight months, so your continued prayers would be most appreciated!

It's great hearing about your courses both at the church and at the community college. Are you considering becoming a counselling Practitioner through CSL? I can see you in that role and imagine you would be an incredible asset to Seattle's spiritual community.

Hard to believe, but it's been over a year since I graduated from the Professional Writing program. Perhaps I told you that the final months consisted of a full-time placement? Many of my classmates were given assigned internships, and a few of us requested or found our own. I wanted to work with an environmental organization and discovered that the Peace and Environment Resource Centre (the PERC) fit the bill perfectly. Just across the canal from our old apartment, it is housed in one big room on the top floor of a three-story red-brick walk-up. The walls are lined with books, periodicals, and stuffed file cabinets. Donated desks and a wild assortment of chairs, computers, and dot-matrix printers are packed between them, all sitting atop ancient green and black asphalt tiles. Diana, my friend and mentor there, is a gentle-hearted redhead with an incredible soprano singing voice who has worked with both adults and kids in non-profits most of her life.

I had so much fun working with her during my placement that I chose to stay on and still volunteer there every week. In addition to organizing and starting to digitize the materials, we produce and distribute a free monthly newspaper, the Peace and Environment News (the PEN) in which my first three published articles are printed! I am also part of the editorial team. Our editor, who is one of the original founders of the

PERC, is the softest-spoken powerhouse I have ever met and has been running this troupe for over *forty years*. Every month she sets a theme for the PEN, and articles pour in from across Canada. I'm grateful for my editing and grammar courses and completely understand your comments about the value of many eyes seeing the same document. It is quite a challenge to put out a sixteen- to twenty-page newspaper with no typos!

While my writing and editing for the PERC is all volunteer work, I am using many of those skills professionally, as well. After graduating and getting my post-grad work permit, I decided to continue tutoring at the college since I had established a steady clientele there. It took a bit of dancing to do so, though. The college rules include the caveat that peer tutors must be enrolled in at least one class. However, my post-grad work permit states very clearly that it is *not* a student permit. So once again I found myself in the middle of a *"you must ..., but you can't ..."* conundrum.

Rolling up my sleeves again, I spent hours sitting on hold and digging through the immigration pages and forums. At last, on my third call to Citizenship and Immigration, I learned that there is an exception! It turns out that one *can* take classes, provided (1) they are off-campus (read: online) and (2) they are not part of a certification program. Good grief!! I cannot *wait* to get through all of these crazy immigration hoops, although

I will admit that my reticence to release the safety net of the college added to this particular predicament.

Regardless, each of the past three semesters I enrolled in a single online class, which allowed me to expand my tutoring hours. I realized before long that even though I was available, students weren't always clamouring for support, and the often-patchy hours meant that I either hung out on campus between appointments – sometimes for hours – or drove the half-hour circuit home and back more than once a day. Combining that with the low wage, cost of online courses, plus the pricey parking permit made for a paltry bottom line. So, in November I began offering private tutoring sessions on Kijiji. It feels great to finally cut the cord from the college. For the first time in almost three years, I am back to being my own boss! And, as much as I love learning, it is really a relief to leave homework and exams behind.

A few other new things have opened up over the past year that I want to tell you about. One of them is my reason for signing off. I'll have to share details another time, but for now Pierre and I are off to a performance; we're the set crew chiefs for Jane Austin's *Pride and Prejudice* at the Ottawa Little Theatre!

I look forward to your next long, newsy email – when you have the time, of course. Meanwhile, please know that you are in my thoughts and prayers, and I'm seeing you living in grace, ease, and perfect health.

With love and blessings always,
Patrice

Chapter 18

December 2013   Ten months later

Standing before the Van Gogh poster pinned to the corkboard on the back wall of my classroom (*my classroom...* the words still rocked me), I reached out to touch the brilliant yellow stars amid swirls of blue.

Starry starry night. Paint your palette blue and grey. Look out on a summer's day, with eyes that know the darkness in my soul... Don McLean's bittersweet lyrics floated through my mind as they had every Tuesday afternoon over the past three months. Briefly, I thought of unpinning, rolling up, and taking the poster home. But no; it belonged in this room.

To my right, a long wall of windows provided liberty from the need for buzzing fluorescent lights. The drab view of the college's air vent and adjacent wing had been a small price to pay for perfect natural light. Three stories below, a lone student trudged through the dirty December snow; a heavy-looking grey scarf draped over her head, following the line of her slumped back. Silently I christened her *Term's End.*

Everything was so quiet. Moments before, the four Professional Writing students I'd coached through fall semester had packed up their laptops for the last time and headed home with a flurry of thanks and promises to stay in touch. Pierre was taking me out for a gourmet birthday dinner this evening, but I wasn't yet ready to surrender the room. The coaching experiment had been successful, and Moira, my former teacher, friend, and now the program coordinator had invited me to coach again next fall. However, the administrative team that assigned classrooms were akin to a multi-member juggling act, doing their best to fulfill preferences and avoid double booking. Union faculty courses took precedence over support staff's needs, so I was low man on the booking list. It was extremely unlikely that I'd end up back in this idyllic space.

As I rearranged the uneven circle of desks and chairs back into lecture hall rows, I felt a familiar juxtaposition of body sensations that often came as doors opened and closed in my life. There was a lump in my throat, melancholy caused not only by the end of the term, but also because *Christmas Belles* had closed at the Little Theatre three nights before. Once again, the backstage ballet was over and new friends were already missed.

That heaviness, though, coexisted with a fluttering anticipation in my chest toward the upcoming chapter.

A few weeks before, my immigration engine had begun to rumble in a completely unexpected turn, so although I wouldn't be at the college or theatre in the coming months, life would certainly not be boring. Since the afternoon's final coaching debriefing had only eaten up a couple of hours, I tucked myself behind the teacher's desk with my thermos of tea and fired up the staff Internet portal to check on recent events.

First stop was the immigration forum. In early October, I had logged in to ask the experts about my alternatives once my post-grad work permit expired in August. A man named Leon, with more than ten thousand positively-rated responses in his history, answered in detail, including links to portions of the Canadian Immigration and Citizenship site I had yet to discover. I scrolled to the top of our thread and re-read his reply to my initial query:

> *Leon:* Do NOT allow your work permit to expire without applying for either a study or visitor's permit. Post-graduate work permits cannot be extended; however, it would behoove you to inquire with the college about the possibility of submitting an LMO, which would allow you to coach next September with a temporary work permit. It's a lengthy and complicated process, so start early.

Once you are married, you have two choices –
apply for Permanent Residence through the Family
class spousal sponsorship via either the *inside-* or
outside-Canada routes. Following the outland
process is probably best, as processing is usually a
few months faster. You can be completely up front
that you are already living in Canada, as long as
your permit status is valid. Just use your current
address as both your and your spouse/sponsor's
mailing and residential address....

After his reply, I had spent hours studying the pros
and cons of inland and outland Permanent Residency
applications and Labour Market Option/work permit
pages. Hoping the requirements wouldn't change
anytime soon, I'd printed out the daunting, booklet-
sized lists of pieces we would need to include with the
applications. Immigration not only needed proof that I
was a healthy, law-abiding woman, but the list of
required and backup documents proving the legitimacy
of Pierre and my relationship filled more than three
pages.

Scrolling down our forum inbox, I re-read Leon's
answers to a couple more questions and then, in the
middle of one of his replies, stood the now-highlighted,
but originally offhanded line

> _Leon:_ … You realize that if you are living with your partner as a couple for at least 12 months or longer, you are already in a common law partnership with him, even though he is not legally divorced, and as such, he could sponsor you right now if you want to.

WHAT?!

Sitting in my classroom, I vividly remembered reading that giant, grammatically awkward sentence the first three or four times, my heart pounding, sweat popping out across my forehead and goosebumps rising all over my body. *Even though he is not legally divorced, he can sponsor me NOW?* I had zipped Leon an instant reply.

> _Patrice:_ Did I read this right?? Would this not be considered bigamy? And if this is true, does it mean that we actually could have applied for my PR nearly *three years ago?*

A minute later his response had arrived.

> _Leon:_ Yes, I guess that's right. Not bigamy.

Pierre and I had laughed and cried, and I began the work of dealing with my frustration around the complexity of this process, the lack of clarity on the ever-changing CIC site, and forgiving myself for not even seeing this as a possibility. But now we knew.

Although it was unlikely according to the posted processing times, we set a goal of obtaining my Permanent Residency before the work permit's expiration date. And so, the race to fulfill the requirements began.

Over the previous eight weeks, I'd booked what seemed like dozens of appointments. First, I chose a doctor from the list of designated medical practitioners whose only job was to see immigration applicants. Their eyes were trained to catch the slightest sign of chronic or contagious diseases. Protecting Canada's socialized medical system was serious business.

After the brief scheduled physical exam performed by a woman with eyes as prodding and icy as her fingers, she handed me four printed pages and barked, "Out, to the left, and down the stairs." There I stood in a crowded hallway queue for three hours (without a book... had I but known!) waiting for a blood draw. Every now and then, hesitant whispers in different languages floated the length of the clinic basement, and at regular intervals a door would open, and a harsh, official voice would bark out, "Next! *Suivant.*"

And then again, we awaited results. Last week, to our great relief, I'd called the doctor's office, received the all-clear, and learned that the official documents had been sent directly to immigration. I checked my Immigration Status Progress Page day after day until at last a green check mark replaced the open box beside "Medical Examination."

A week after the exam I booked a fingerprinting appointment and mailed the inked form along with the application for my FBI police certificate to the states, proving I was not a law-breaker. The timeline for this step was tricky. Its timestamp could not exceed three months before the Permanent Residency application date, and the FBI's website stated up to a four-month processing period. Every afternoon I sorted through our stack of mail looking for an official FBI return address. So far, nothing had appeared.

Taking a swallow of my tepid tea, I glanced out the window and saw the orange tint fading as dusk came on. I thought of the hours of paperwork still to complete. By far the most time-consuming portion of the application has been gathering our historic details and proof that Pierre and my relationship is "sincere and ongoing." Every few days I have added to the growing stack in the folder: tax forms, insurance and banking statements, copies of theatre programs with Pierre and I listed as co-chiefs, and page after page of dated photographs. We are still awaiting letters from my folks, Aunt Jeannine, and three friends – two from Seattle, and Val, of course.

My email-hoarding tendencies came in handy here, as one of my Outlook files was filled with love notes from our long-distance days. Scrolling through them, I realized with a jolt that most of our recent emails contained grocery requests and updates on work schedules; written endearments have become sparse as the years have passed. Wanting to rectify that, I shot him a quick email, letting him know I'd be home soon and thanking him for making reservations at the Wellington Gastropub for my birthday dinner. "Can't wait to spend the evening celebrating with you, sweetheart. Love, The Luckiest Woman in the World."

Logging out of Algonquin's system, I shut the computer down, drained the last of my tea, and with one last look around, bade my room farewell. Twenty minutes later I stomped the snow off my boots and bustled in our front door. "Honey, I'm home!" I called, hanging my coat and scarf in the entry closet. Copper grinned goofily around his favourite stuffed woobie, his tail rhythmically whacking the entry table. Penny wove under his belly and between my legs as I set my dripping boots on the entry mat.

I could hear Pierre's muffled voice behind his office door, evidently on the phone. His tone was low and serious; it was clearly not one of his racing buddies, more likely a business call. After washing out my thermos, I settled into Gramps' rocker and gave Cop a nice, long ear-rub, reaching to scratch Penny's back as she wove figure-eights in front of us. After a few minutes of silence from the office, the door slowly creaked opened and Pierre joined me in the living room, holding a printed document.

"What's this?" I asked, glancing briefly at it, and then looking up at him. "Sorry for interrupting your call when I came in. Who were you talking to?"

He hesitated a moment and then said, "It was my lawyer." With brows raised and eyes locked on the sheet in his hand, he continued, "She sent this over a while ago, then called immediately after." Handing me the page, he continued in a hesitant, stunned-sounding voice, "Happy birthday, my love. It is finally over."

"You're *serious?*" Reading carefully through the signed divorce papers, my eyes filled up in overwhelm and relief. *Best birthday, ever!* Wiping away tears, I looked up and saw that Pierre, too, was pulling a tissue from his pocket to dry his eyes. He had a soft smile on his face.

"So," he said, his words slow and husky. "I have to go to court next month for the judge's approval, but once that's done, how about we get married?"

Saying Yes

Chapter 19

March 2014   Three months later

I woke up at 2:30 a.m. in a full sweat, tossed for half an hour, mind galloping; finally, I tip-toed out to the living room, hoping a cup of Sleepytime tea would live up to its name. After the first cup, my thoughts still whirled. *What if I forget something? Is there enough gas in the car?* And *If I don't wind down soon, I'll never make it through tomorrow!*

Funny, I felt no hesitation or nervousness about the upcoming service itself. My mind just wouldn't stop processing all the recent events. After reading the same page five times, I set aside my book and wandered back into the kitchen to add a second bag and more hot water to the teapot. Carrying it back to my rocker, I opened my laptop to my journal document. I was dismayed to see that it had been nearly three months since I'd added an entry. Perhaps pouring all these thoughts out in writing would help. It had worked on far less important occasions than tonight's. And I *really* needed to sleep. After all, no one wants to look worn out in their wedding photos.

Tucking my fuzzy blanket under the computer and feeling Copper settle at my feet, the memories of the past few months arose, and my fingers began their dance across the keyboard.

Journal Entry – March 13, 2014

The evening of December 30, 2013, Pierre and I met with a notary, a lawyer who worked from his huge glass-topped kitchen table at his Britannia Beach home. Officially signing the Common-Law Declaration was our last step in collecting the necessary documents to apply for Permanent Residency. The following day – New Year's Eve – I added that form to the two-inch stack of paperwork, making certain everything was complete and in order, made copies for my file, then addressed the giant manila envelope. Before sealing it, I tucked in what I hoped would be the clincher: a letter explaining that while Pierre and I were currently common-law partners, we intended to marry within a few months; I would send our marriage certificate once it arrived.

We snapped a couple of selfies holding the thick envelope, shed a few tears of relief and hope, and drove the weighty packet to the post office together on the final day of the year. A few days later, January 3rd, my immigration site's progress page had a new notation: "Application Received." The first phase – expected to take a month or so – was the immigration office's review of Pierre's documentation, proving that he was eligible to sponsor me. My portion of the packet, according to the immigration website, was expected to take an additional fourteen months for processing.

On February 3rd, exactly one month after CIC received the application, Pierre's approval of sponsorship arrived in the mail – just five days after the long-awaited finalization of his divorce. Since most of our evenings were filled with Crew Chief duties for *Pride and Prejudice* at the theatre, we celebrated these momentous events in the Green Room, glasses raised with the high-spirited cast and crew.

Over the years we had been discussing wedding plans and were in complete agreement on so many aspects. Since our first wedding ceremonies had been exciting but stressful, we had neither the need for, nor the desire to repeat that theatrical ritual. I was ready for the waiting to be over, however, so once it was actually possible, I began planning in earnest. What to wear? No to a traditional wedding gown, but yes to a dress. No to white, but yes to any other colour – including black, the one we eventually chose. No need for a tux, but yes to a jacket and tie. Our rings had been designed and made months before and sat waiting in a bedside drawer.

We wanted it simple, so the venue we fell back on was City Hall. As the timing of the event became more imminent, though, I began to struggle with the idea of a cold, government-based proceeding. I wanted the memory of our wedding day to be full of warmth and gentleness; the idea of hearing "next" and "sign here," stamp, stamp, stamp, brought a feeling of emptiness, so unlike the deep connection that we felt and a wimpy culmination to these long years of perseverance.

I thought back to the customized, cherished wedding ceremonies my ex-husband, ordained online through the Universal Life Church, had performed for friends over the years. *Of course! We could find someone to officiate!* Back to Kijiji I went, amazed to find more than two dozen ads for wedding officiants. Some offered traditional church weddings, while others provided rented halls, or outdoor ceremonies in gothic, Harley, or Renaissance themes. There were people who specialized in rustic garden parties and string-quartet-included ultra-luxurious events.

When I scrolled through Reverend Vivian London's website, I had a feeling she might be right for us, and after a short conversation on the phone, I knew she was. A soft-spoken lady, perhaps ten years our senior, she held ceremonies either in her home—a short drive from ours—or at a location of our choice. Pierre had no preference, but I wanted our wedding to take place in its own unique setting rather than blending in with everything else in our home. The posted photos of Vivian's living room showed light lavender walls, white roses and lace, and subtle flowered pastel paintings. It looked elegant and cozy and not at all fussy… just the feeling I was hoping for. She understood our desire for a simple, spiritual but not religious ceremony. During long conversations over the years, Pierre and I had committed to many of our values: keeping our relationship honourable, passionate, and intimate, vowing to repel the poisonous taking-each-other-for-granted habit, and holding each other's hearts with the utmost care and respect. Neither of us felt the need to have others witness those oaths, so were content with the Reverend's short, standard script.

Her home accommodated up to a dozen guests, but we had already decided that we wanted only a few witnesses. Pierre invited his oldest friend, Charlie, to be his best man, and since I couldn't choose between Vickie and Val, we asked them both. Vickie to sign as my witness and Val to record the service. We would throw a big back-yard party once the snow was gone. We booked the wedding day for a Friday afternoon in mid-March, giving ourselves what I thought would be plenty of time to get all of the paperwork completed. Knowing what I know now, I chuckled; perhaps I should have chosen June.

Roused by my quiet snicker, Copper lifted his sleepy-eyed white muzzle and rose slowly to his feet. He stared intently at me, his way of saying that a trip to the backyard would be appreciated. Setting my computer aside, I let him out and watched from the window as he followed the well-stomped path through the snow and around the yard. I laughed again, thinking of yesterday's antics.

Since living here, we have gone through four different purportedly squirrel-proof bird feeders. The only one that foiled the rodents was discovered, destroyed, and licked clean by a bear who found her way out of the greenbelt last spring. Rather than taking the wise route and replacing it with the same model, I fell for a competitor's marketing.

Our latest purchase was a six-inch diameter, eighteen-inch tall vertical tube surrounded by a wire cage, which we hung from the back fence. It was out there in the dark, completely empty of black sunflower seeds, even though I filled it only two days ago. The ultimate insult to the chickadees, sparrows, and other finches (not to mention us) came yesterday afternoon, in the form of a young grey squirrel whose photo I snapped. The little critter wasn't content with swiping the seeds from the bottom tray through the cage as its brothers and sisters had done. No, it had squeezed through the wire squares and was lounging on the tray *inside* the cage, feasting constantly for more than an hour. Amazingly, it was eventually able to wedge itself out, despite its round cheeks and belly. Almost nothing, it seemed, would stop the squirrels when it came to these treats.

A moment later, Copper's whine brought me back to the present. I let him in, dried his feet, and replenished my tea. We resumed our respective spots on and beside Gramps' rocker, and again I began to type.

With so many milestones behind us: Permanent Residency in the works, Pierre's divorce finalized, and our wedding date set, I thought the major struggles were over. And then I printed out the list of required pre-wedding documents, including their steps and timelines. Pierre's initial response was to move the wedding date out a few weeks. However, it looked to me as if we had at least two weeks' play. "If everything goes right," I responded, "we should have plenty of time." He smiled and let me get to it.

The biggest complication was once again that blasted border. Since I had gone through a "foreign divorce," I had to first provide certified divorce documents from the Kitsap County courthouse in Washington State. They then had to be sent – along with something called a Legal Opinion Letter (a local lawyer's opinion that the divorce documents were genuine) – to the Registrar's Office in Thunder Bay, Ontario, for authorization. Once processed, they would return my original divorce documents and an authorization decree freeing us to obtain our Ontario marriage license.

Unfortunately, I was told, Kitsap County could not mail, fax, or email certified divorce documents. I had to "pop into the courthouse" and pick up a copy… no matter that I was 2600 miles away. Yes, they eventually said, I could commission a friend to purchase it for me on weekdays between 8:00 AM and noon or 1:00 and 4:00 PM. Since nearly all my friends worked, and the trip from Seattle to the courthouse in Port Orchard took four hours round trip without traffic, my options were limited. Then, ah ha! Gerry and Jenny, my golden-retriever community friends, lived less than an hour from Port Orchard – and Gerry had recently retired! Happy to help, he not only procured the documents the next morning, but sent them via overnight courier and refused reimbursement, writing, "Consider this our wedding gift."

Two afternoons later, I sat in a young lawyer's downtown office answering detailed questions about my former husband, my fiancé, and me. Legal Opinion Letters were not common, it turned out, and as this was her first time filing one, it took *three times* for her to get all of the details right. The notarized letter and divorce documents were snail-mailed to Thunder Bay, since the Registrar's office required originals. A few days after they arrived the first time, the lawyer called, apologizing, saying she'd juxtaposed "my gentlemen's names," and would I come back in to sign a corrected one. I did, and again she mailed the letter.

A week later, another call came in; this time, she had used my ex's return address rather than ours on the letter, and it needed correction *again*. I admit to being far less patient with her than I'd been at our first two meetings. The last mailing was finally mistake-free, but somehow, once it arrived at the Registrar General's office, it disappeared.

After making at least a dozen phone calls to various departments, I raced back to the contrite lawyer's office last Friday and practically tore a *fourth*, signed copy from her hand. Dashing home, I wrote a cover letter outlining the previous weeks' events and requesting expedited processing. A printed copy of Reverend Vivian's emailed confirmation of our wedding date served as the required "proof of urgency." Included also were the fax and phone numbers of a clerk at the Kanata Service Centre where we would purchase our marriage license. In the event the hard copies didn't arrive on time, that helpful manager was willing to make an exception. If necessary, she would accept an emergency fax of authorization and a phone call from the Registrar's office verbally confirming the authenticity of my divorce documents.

Back in my car, I ran this packet of pages to the Purolator courier's office, sending it overnight, and praying that the authorization decree would make its way back to us within a few days. The stars finally aligned. Wednesday, a day and a half ago – just forty-eight hours before our wedding was scheduled – a courier knocked on the door and delivered the authorization decree from Thunder Bay. I nearly collapsed with relief

... until we couldn't locate Pierre's certificate of divorce.

We practically tore the house apart for forty-five minutes, with me sobbing, moaning, crying out, *This can NOT be happening! Not after all we have gone through.* Pierre systematically went through every pile of paper in his office, stopping to hug me, bring me tissue, and reassure me that we would find it. At last, the single sheet appeared in a nicely organized stack on Pierre's living room end table. We had *both* thumbed through those papers, but obviously not carefully enough. And there it was. Wrapping me in his arms, Pierre held me as my intense sobs of frustration turned to quiet tears of release and exhaustion.

Yesterday morning we drove to the Kanata Service Centre, a modern green glass building just a minute's drive from Reverend Vivian's house, where we thanked the manager for being willing to bend the rules for us, had we needed it. A smiling woman named Nancy led us to a tiny conference room and walked us through the process. Less than an hour later, giddy with relief, we were sipping tea and coffee and eating breakfast sandwiches at a neighbourhood café, marriage license safely tucked deep into my purse. Ten hours from now, we will hand that paper to Reverend Vivian, and the rest of our lives together will begin.

Closing my journal document and the cover of my laptop, I set it aside and reached down to pull sweet Copper-top's head onto my lap. *Think it's time to head back to bed, buddy?* I asked him, yawning and scratching behind his downy ears. *Tomorrow's the big day.* His warm brown eyes blinked slowly, and we stood and walked down the hall toward the soft sound of my favourite lullaby.

Epilogue

A month after our wedding, another packet arrived from the Registrar General's office containing official copies of our Certificate of Marriage. Stapling a copy to a few wedding photos, I mailed our updated marital status to the immigration office the next morning.

It was mid-April, and their website estimated another full *year* of processing for my Permanent Residency. I immediately began chanting up a shorter timeline, enlisting the help of both local and online friends. Every day I pictured myself growing old with my dear Pierre in Canada.

Standing at the kitchen counter a little more than two months later, I opened another official-looking envelope from Citizenship and Immigration.

A full *ten months* before its projected arrival, my Confirmation of Permanent Residence was in my hands! Pierre swung me around laughing and singing "Oh Happy Day!" A second enclosed page explained that, to finalize the process, sometime over the next five months I had to leave the country. Upon re-entry, a border officer would authorize my landing, and I would be a confirmed Permanent Resident.

Naturally, my inclination was to drive to the States the next day. Pierre's work and my tutoring schedule didn't allow that, but when I realized that Canada Day was only eleven days out, I pushed for going as soon as possible. I wanted to dance with Pierre and hundreds of thousands of other Canadians on Parliament Hill, celebrating the country's birthday and the fact that it was now officially my home.

The following week, Pierre and I booked an afternoon off and drove back to the border. Once in New York, we made a U-turn at the first stop sign, drove back across the Saint Lawrence River bridge, and parked at the Canadian crossing. Inside, an expressionless officer explained that Immigration was in the process of changing computer systems. Not finding my name on his screen, he said, "We have the old version of the system. Your confirmation doesn't show up, so evidently it was input into the new one. We are unable to process your landing. Contact CIC in Ottawa and schedule an appointment when the new system is in place… in four to six weeks."

No!! I felt Pierre's hand tuck under my elbow as I faltered a step back. Everything in me wanted to yank that monitor around and search the list myself, but of course that wouldn't have been wise. Tears rose up again as I asked if he would check once more. My name was not there. He was kind enough to write a memo confirming our border crossing so that we might avoid another two-hour drive. Handing me the note and my documents, he turned away.

Back home, I wrote a post to my Facebook community, again asking for prayers for a MUCH quicker timeline than four to six weeks. Half a dozen phone calls to the city-centre CIC office and Ottawa airport's border office combined with the power of collective visualization worked its magic.

At 11:00 AM on July 8, 2014 – just twelve days after our trip to the border – Pierre met me downtown at the immigration office. I presented my certification letter, the note from the border officer, and personal identification to a smiling CIC officer. I signed the authorization under her signature, hugged and hugged and hugged my happy husband, and posed for a beaming photograph. At long last, I was a permanent resident of the "glorious and free" country of Canada and no one could separate me from the love of my life.

Eleven days later in our newly landscaped back yard, we stood with fifty loved ones – including my parents and (surprise!) my sister and brother-in-law – nibbling exotic dishes catered by one of my former students. Raising glasses of champagne and sparkling cider, we toasted, "To Pierre and Patrice. To friends and family. And to love."

December 7, 2018   Three and a half years later

I, along with seventy-nine other people – toddlers to grandparents from countries all over the world – took our final immigration step. Witnessed by my fabulous Canadian family and friends, I pledged my oath to the Crown and with misty eyes became a dual citizen.

To my beloved Pierre and each of you who encouraged and/or celebrated this journey with me, I thank you for your love and support. Every single day I am grateful for this incredible life.   And so it is.

THE END

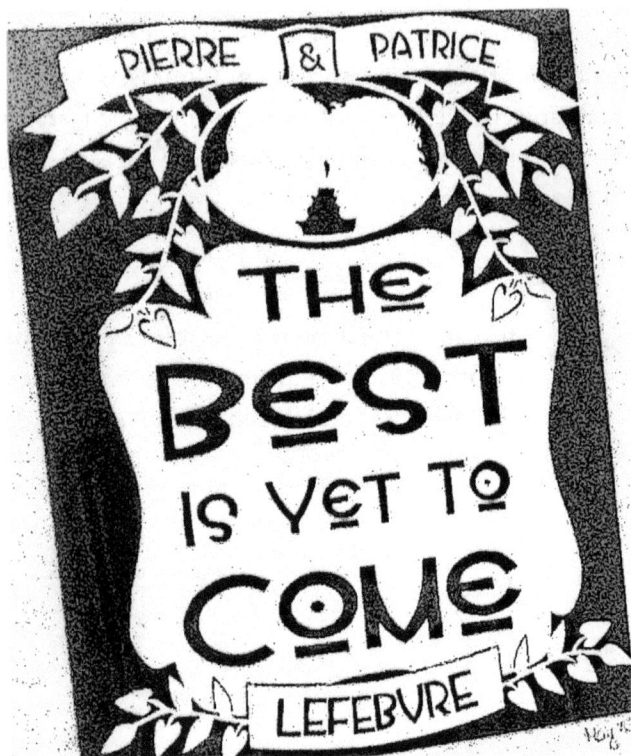

*Papercut designed and created by Sharon Presseault

About the Author

Photo by Alan Dean
Ottawa Little Theatre headshot

Patrice Lefebvre lives in Ottawa, Ontario, with her husband, Pierre, and their adopted (and slightly spoiled) fuzzers, Penny and Kimchi. In addition to helping adults and youth improve their communication skills, she presents workshops and provides happiness and fulfillment coaching based on Mike Dooley's program and book, *Infinite Possibilities.* Her greatest joy (second only to living with the love of her life) is empowering others to say "YES!" and supporting them as they create the lives of their dreams.

If you enjoyed my debut book, *Saying Yes*, and think others might too, I would be deeply grateful if you would help spread the word about it by posting a quick review.

Many thanks!
Patrice

www.ingramcontent.com/pod-product-compliance
Lightning Source LLC
LaVergne TN
LVHW051403080426
835508LV00022B/2954